THE
GREAT FAMILY
WINE ESTATES
OF FRANCE

THE
GREAT FAMILY
WINE ESTATES
OF FRANCE

STYLE • TRADITION • HOME

SOLVI DOS SANTOS

TEXT BY FLORENCE BRUTTON

292 color illustrations

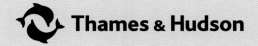

Thames & Hudson

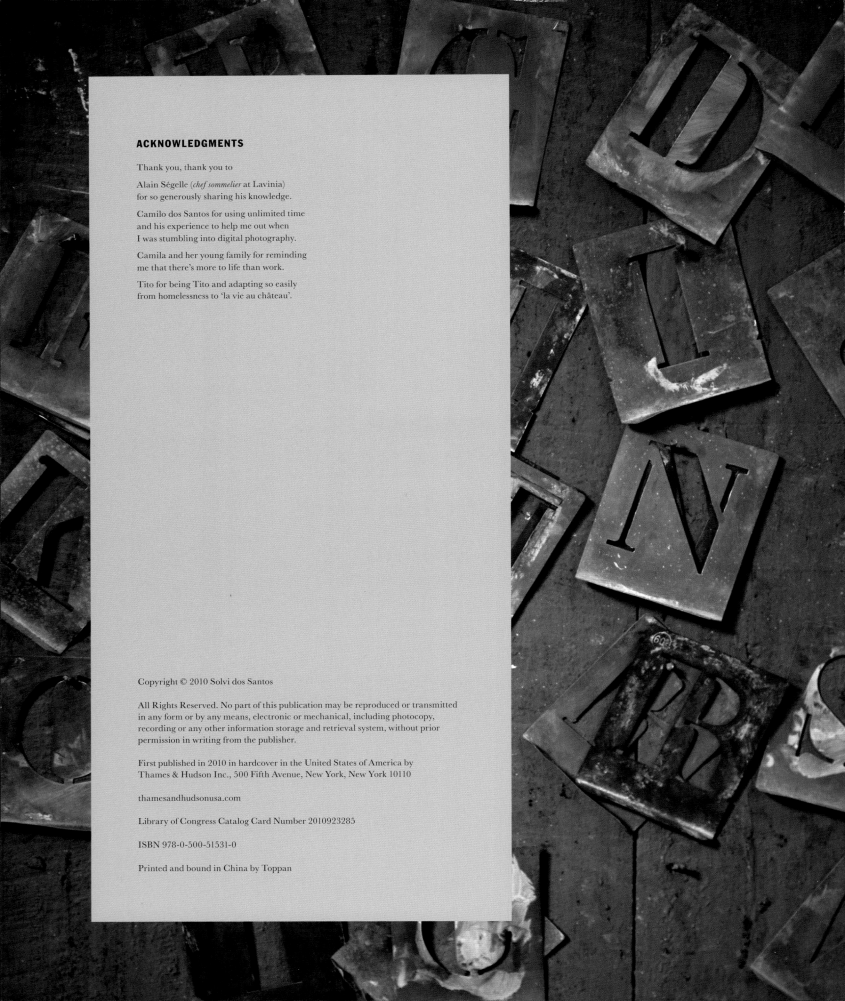

ACKNOWLEDGMENTS

Thank you, thank you to

Alain Ségelle (*chef sommelier* at Lavinia)
for so generously sharing his knowledge.

Camilo dos Santos for using unlimited time
and his experience to help me out when
I was stumbling into digital photography.

Camila and her young family for reminding
me that there's more to life than work.

Tito for being Tito and adapting so easily
from homelessness to 'la vie au château'.

First published in 2010 in hardcover in the United States of America by
Thames & Hudson Inc., 500 Fifth Avenue, New York, New York 10110

thamesandhudsonusa.com

Library of Congress Catalog Card Number 2010923285

ISBN 978-0-500-51531-0

Printed and bound in China by Toppan

CONTENTS

INTRODUCTION

Great commercial enterprises of every kind have their great houses. All bear witness to their moment in history, but none are so intimately linked to the land they occupy as the family-owned châteaux featured in these pages. Here, the house that celebrates the business stands at the very heart of its land. The vines come right to the door.

Wine is synonymous with France and French culture, in a manner that has no equivalent among other nations. In truth, Italy makes more wine than France, and Spain has a greater vineyard area. Greece, Germany, Switzerland, Hungary, Morocco and Algeria all have a historic tradition of wine production, and the New World is building a tradition of its own – California, Chile and Australia, to mention just three. But these other countries offer nothing like the choice of wine from France, and their national reputation is often attached to just one type: retsina from Greece, for instance, or Tokay from Hungary. France, by contrast, is famous as the home of wine in general and the etiquette that goes with it. Wine is central to the French *art de vivre*, and it has largely defined French human geography. The map of France is built around vineyards.

Vines have been growing in France for more than two thousand years. First introduced by the Greeks, they were cultivated with abandon by the Romans who drank wine with every meal. Indeed, such was the proliferation of vineyards in France that in 51 BC all new plantings were banned by imperial decree for almost 200 years. Thereafter, the Romans established vineyards throughout France, starting in the Rhône Valley. Invading barbarian hordes from the 5th century onwards then trampled rough shod over the Roman heritage, vines included. The Catholic Church, however, most notably the bishops, had a God-given duty to safeguard Christian tradition, wine included. Consecrated wine became central to the Catholic dogma of transubstantiation – the belief that bread and wine are transformed into the body and blood of Christ at Holy Communion – and winegrowers became men with a divine purpose – monks mostly, first the Benedictines, followed in the 12th century by their more austere brothers, the Cistercians. There are currently 100 named vineyards in France that were founded by the monasteries. The Abbaye de Valmagne, for instance (see pages 192–97), to mention but one.

Wine production in the early Middle Ages was ruled by the feudal social structure. Vineyards were owned by the nobility-clergy and worked by the peasants in exchange for the lord's protection – a custom known as noblesse oblige. Charlemagne planted vines, as did the first Capetian kings, most notably in the

Opposite: The lavabo-fountain in the cloister garden of the former Cistercian Abbey of Valmagne, one of only two remaining in France. According to the Rule of Saint Bénédict, every abbey had to include a fountain where the monks could purify their hands before prayer or meals (touching bread with soiled hands was strictly forbidden, in memory of Christ's Last Supper). This one is located outside the refectory, its soothing waters adding to the charms of a cloister garden that was the monks' only contact with natural greenery. The austere Cistercians insisted on self-sufficiency, embracing a cloistered existence until death.

precinct of the Louvre Palace in Paris. In the 14th century the Avignon Papacy established vineyards in the southern Rhône region, an area now known as Châteauneuf-du-Pape (literally 'new castle of the pope'). The Duchy of Burgundy became famous for the excellence of its vineyards, tended by Cistercian monks under the protection of the powerful dukes of Burgundy. This pattern was repeated across France. Then in the 15th century winegrowing ceased to be an exclusively noble prerogative, opening its doors to the ruling bourgeoisie. So commenced a tradition of family winegrowing that carried lofty status – to say nothing of its lucrative potential. Winegrowing denoted wealth, patrician values and a commitment to family land.

Every one of the estates in this book is marked by a keen sense of heritage and patrimony, rooted in their particular locality. It is no surprise that France was first to devise the concept of 'place of origin protection', as enshrined in the French system of appellation d'origine contrôlée (AOC). French culture, like wine itself, is much more than just the sum of its parts. Regions are to France what grapes are to wine: the keys to identity. Whether in Champagne or the Loire Valley, in the Languedoc or Corsica, each of the estates featured here stands as a declaration of France's precious diversity, and the local customs and skills that sustain it. France, traditional home of wine and gastronomy, is a champion of local production. Nowhere is this more apparent than in French wines, and the individuality for which they are famed.

At the heart of it all is the concept of *terroir* – a uniquely French term for the natural and man-made conditions that define each particular plot of cultivated land. To every vineyard, its own distinctive wines. As French writer Colette once said, 'only the vine can accurately convey the real taste of the earth.' And no other form of cultivation is a greater test of man's skills.

All of the estates in this book display an aversion to sameness and standardization, and a devotion to those precious qualities that distinguish their *terroir* from all others. They are the loudest champions of the eco-friendly practices that are key to sustainable agriculture everywhere. It is little wonder that they are so staunchly opposed to the standardizing influence of globalization.

'Where wine goes, goes the world,' said Jonathan Nossiter, sometime sommelier and award-winning film director of the controversial wine documentary *Mondovino*. And happily for France, that world seems increasingly inclined to turn its back on mass production and mass appeal.

Vive la différence!

THE LOIRE VALLEY

CHÂTEAU DE VAUGAUDRY

'Picrochole and his men, thinking all was lost, took to their heels and fled in a panic. Gargantua chased them almost as far as Vaugaudry, killing and slaying all the way before sounding the retreat.' It is now some 450 years since French Renaissance writer and local boy François Rabelais (*c.* 1494–1553) wrote these lines, and Château de Vaugaudry no longer stands where it stood then. The property was rebuilt in the late 1800s, relocated some 100 yards west of its original location. And all because its then owner, a French senator called Achille Joubert (1814–83), wanted a better view of Château Chinon. A splendid example of Gargantuan self-indulgence – particularly since Chinon had by that time suffered two centuries of neglect at the hands of Cardinal Richelieu's descendants…

'Joubert was a wealthy horse dealer, the equivalent of today's car salesman,' says present owner Antoine Belloy. Joubert also built the wall surrounding the property, enclosing some 58 hectares of vines that had produced wine since Rabelais' day. The establishment of the *clos* coincided with the arrival of the railway linking Chinon to Loudun (a place immortalized by Aldous Huxley in *The Devils of Loudun* – but that's another story). Sadly, none of this compensated for Joubert's extravagance, which was also not helped by *Phylloxera Vastatrix* and repeated changes of ownership. The property acquired in 1949 by Antoine's grandfather Dr Bonnet boasted 58 hectares of … apple orchards, with not a vine in sight. And so it remained until the doctor's demise in 1978 when his daughter Françoise Belloy (Antoine's mother) took matters in hand – and cleared roughly half of the orchards for vines.

The estate today boasts some 12 hectares of Cabernet Franc plantings, which 'perform better than ever thanks to global warming,' says Antoine. The vineyards are planted in a single block, separated from the house itself by a manicured lawn punctuated by box shrubs. At the back of the house rises a steep hillside of dense deciduous woodlands. The setting is as visually lyrical as you would expect of the Touraine, home of the greatest of all the Loire châteaux – Chambord, Chenonceau and Cheverney, to mention but three. Balzac, Descartes, Ronsard and Rabelais were all born in this area. Leonardo da Vinci spent his last years here.

It is perhaps fitting in this cradle of the French Renaissance that Château de Vaugaudry should undergo a renaissance of its own. Wine production is once again a priority, but the house remains the much-loved country retreat of the Belloy family – Antoine and his wife and two daughters. A banker by profession, Antoine divides his time between Vaugaudry and Paris – 'once a two-hour drive, now three due to speed restrictions.' He describes himself as the château's 'treasurer and managing director', always deferring to the winemaking expertise of Philippe Montigny, his maître de chais of some 15 years' standing. A man of figures he may be, but Antoine Belloy has a way with words. The vines today, he says, have that serenity and wisdom that come with age, producing youthful, sinewy wines with a succulent core of fruit. Rabelais, the first to speak of Chinon's 'raspberry-tasting' wine, couldn't have put it better.

The house faces north, away from the sun, looking across its vineyards and all the way to Château Chinon (roughly a mile away). A grand rebuilding by its 19th-century owner, Achille Joubert, featured among other things two impressive stone terraces, one at the basement utility level and one above.

Preceding pages: The 'grand salon' (main reception room) opens onto the top terrace, via the three pairs of French windows in the centre of the façade.

Opposite: 'Grand salon', with the 'petit salon' visible through the doors. Furnishings and interior decoration are typical 18th century, reflecting the tastes of the elder Mme Belloy. Featured here, against the wall, is a Style Régence (1700–30) *commode en tombeau*, so named for its sarcophagus-like design. Being north-facing, the 'grand salon' never sees any sun, its shady light enhancing the sombre lustre of this magnificent gold-framed mirror.

Right: Art Deco wrought-iron mirror coat rack, originating from Dr Bonnet's house in the Loir-et-Cher department (north central France). It stands today under the magnificent Imperial stone staircase (two symmetrical flights that come together at the first landing).

Above: 'Captain chair' on the terrace outside the billiard room.

Opposite, above, left: Vaugaudry corks, the smaller ones for red, the larger cork in the centre (2008) from a rosé.

Opposite, above, right: Magnums of Vaugaudry red.

Opposite, below, left: Close-up of armchair fabric in one of the main reception rooms.

Opposite, below, right: Oak *barriques bordelaises* (seasoned Bordeaux barrels) used for the old-vines bottling. Cuvée du Clos du Plessis-Gerbault, Vaugaudry's other red wine, is aged in stainless steel tanks for two to eight years.

CHÂTEAU DE BRISSAC

Château de Brissac is the tallest château in France, and the most gloriously original. The immense towers that flank it to north and south are all that remains of the original 15th-century castle, and the subsequent rebuild was never completed. The works undertaken in 1606 by Charles II de Cossé, First Duke of Brissac, came to a halt with his unexpected death in 1621. His son Louis then cancelled the project and the castle today remains as it was when workmen downed tools nearly 400 years ago – unfinished due to lack of funds. Hence the asymmetrical façade, dominated by a five-storey, 154 ft (47 m) high donjon that should mark the centre of the eastern elevation but doesn't.

Stately homes are not cheap to run and this one is no exception – as one might expect of a castle known as the 'Colossus of the Val de Loire'. But it is definitely 'home' first and 'stately' second, seat and hub of the Brissac dynasty since 1502, when the château and name that went with it were acquired by Anjou nobleman René de Cossé. So began the 'family adventure' that is pursued today by the very genial Charles-André de Cossé, Marquis and future 14th Duke of Brissac. He has managed this estate 'full time' since 1986, with time off in 1993 to marry Larissa, a Hungarian-born aristocrat who danced her way into the Royal Ballet and ultimately into his heart. 'The men provide continuity, but it is the chatelaine, as wife and mother, who rings the changes.' Larissa, he says, is a chatelaine in the finest Brissac tradition. Memorable predecessors include French sugar heiress Jeanne Say who in the 19th century brought the château back from the brink of ruin after the French Revolution. She too had a taste for the footlights – which she indulged by building her very own theatre in her very own castle. The auditorium survives today, perched on the two top floors of the château, a plush velvet tribute to a gifted soprano who refused to be silenced by rank.

Charles-André and his family occupy private quarters on the second floor – a mere fraction of this 86,000 sq ft (8,000 sq m), 204-room monument that welcomes nearly 50,000 visitors a year. His aim, noblesse oblige, is to send visitors home 'feeling that they've had a good day out.' His model is England's Goodwood House and estate, Brissac's twin of some 30 years standing – 'charming parklands seen through rain-washed sunlight.' So it is that Brissac now boasts an English tea room, the latest in a string of attractions that do, of course, include vineyards. What would the landscapes of the Loire be without vines?

'Every new generation breathes new life into these old stones,' says Charles-André who, like his own father and his father before him, grew up in the château. And like his own children today, he attended the local schools. Now it is his turn to stand in one of these towers and see them off to school 'checking that they haven't forgotten anything.' One of five siblings himself, he has four children of his own, one boy (the eldest) and three girls. He says he never planned to succeed his father – 'it just turned out that way' – and his own son may well say the same some day. Places like Château de Brissac have a will of their own.

The 'grand salon', originally known as the *salon doré* (gilded salon) after its gold leaf 17th-century coffered ceiling. The linked 'c' motif was the monogram of Charles de Cossé, whose bust features in the monumental, Louis XIII-style fireplace. The chandeliers are Murano Venetian crystal, two of four in the salon. To the right are portraits of the 12th Duke of Brissac and his Duchess (Charles-André's grandparents) by French designer and illustrator Bernard Boutet de Monvel (1884–1949).

Above: The asymmetrical eastern façade, featuring the massive 15th-century towers that were the only bits still standing after the French Wars of Religion (1562–98). Rebuilding works undertaken by Charles de Cossé were cut short by his death in 1621, 'leaving a partially built 17th-century castle, within a partially destroyed 15th-century castle.' Laszlo, the Marquis's eldest son, has his bedroom in one of these towers.

Right: Main entrance doorknocker, fondly remembered by the Marquis from his school days in the village. 'Hammering on the door was our only way in, since none of us had keys.'

Right: The main entrance hall, displaying yellowish-white tuffeau limestone (from the Latin *tofus*, meaning spongy stone). The property straddles the Paris Basin (Loire Valley tuffeau) and the Massif Armoricain (Anjou slate and schist); the vineyards are exclusively located in the Anjou AOC. The crest over the doorway to the kitchen depicts historic Brissac alliances. The matching tables with barley-twist legs are Louis XIII.

Overleaf: The portrait gallery on the first floor. In the centre is the only known portrait of famous Champagne widow 'La Veuve Clicquot', who is shown here in a work by French artist Léon Coignet, with her great-granddaughter at her feet. The room faces east, enjoying fine natural light but looks particularly resplendent when illuminated by its magnificent chandelier.

Above: The bedchamber where Louis XIII slept at the time he made short-lived peace with his mother, Marie de Médicis, in 1620 after three years of war. The treaty was known as the Paix d'Angers (Peace of Angers), but was actually signed in Brissac where the king stayed for three much-celebrated days. But Marie's 'real stroke of genius', says the Marquis, was to discover her protégé Cardinal Richelieu…

Right: The castle chapel, next to the portrait gallery, housed in one of the 15th-century towers. Featured here is an ornate, Italian Renaissance seigneurial bench, brought back from Naples in the 19th century by a former Duchess of Brissac. The chapel is particularly charming, boasting some very fine bas-reliefs by celebrated French sculptor Pierre-Jean David (1788–1856), better known as David d'Angers (after his birthplace).
.

Above: Louis XIII's
bedchamber, featuring a
collection of tapestries based
on 17th-century master
painter Charles Lebrun's
'Battles of Alexander the
Great' series for Versailles.
On either side of the
canopied bed are two carved
Italian Renaissance cabinets,
with secret compartments
and drawers. Essential, one
imagines, with a mother like
Marie de Médicis.

Opposite: The billiard
room, at the entrance to
the private theatre built
by 19th-century sugar
heiress and gifted soprano,
Jeanne Say, Marquise of
Brissac. The half-vaulting
is characteristic of the
château's interior. On the
wall is a portrait of the
10th Duchess of Brissac
by 19th-century painter
Steuben.

CHÂTEAU DE COULAINE

When Etienne de Bonnaventure was a child in the 1960s, Château de Coulaine looked out over lush pastures dotted with grazing cattle and fields of cereal crops punctuated by vines. Cradled between the rivers Loire and Vienne, the Véron region is a farmer's paradise – a land of ancient *bocage* with flood meadows bordered by hedgerows of coppiced ash. Etienne's childhood years were every boy's dream – cycling alone to school in Chinon, summer bathing in the river Vienne and bareback riding with his friend Philippe. Château de Coulaine was nature's own playground. 'It made Etienne what he is today,' says his wife Pascale. 'A born and bred son of the soil, viscerally attached to the land and the house of his ancestors.' Pascale's own childhood was the complete opposite of her husband's. She grew up by the sea, the daughter of a naval medical officer who shuttled his family from one duty station to another. As a restorer of fine art, she originally came to Chinon in search of work – which she found, along with a husband and a way of life that 'more than compensates for the absence of salt water.'

Etienne's forebears were no strangers to the sea themselves. In 1632 they were among the first French settlers in Quebec, eventually returning with the new name of 'Bonnaventure' after their homestead on the Ile-Bonnaventure in the Gulf of Saint Lawrence. It was their ancestor, the salaciously named Jehan de Guarguessalles (meaning 'salty throat'), who acquired Château de Coulaine, through marriage, in 1300. The property has remained in the same family ever since, then and now planted with vines. Wine production has continued here for 700 years, and probably since Gallo-Roman times when the site was home to the 'Villa Colonia' (origin of the name 'Coulaine'). But the château as François Rabelais knew it is very different today. Rebuilt in around 1460 to 1470 by Jehan's grandson, the structure is unchanged since the 15th century. The neo-Gothic style however is 19th century, after the manner of fashionable French architect Viollet-le-Duc. The grounds and parklands also date from that period, a nod to English landscape gardener Lancelot 'Capability' Brown, with follies and perspectives galore. The vineyard has been quite literally reborn: some 20 hectares of organically grown vines now in production, including eight *en fermage*. In just over 20 years, Etienne de Bonnaventure has established an estate after his own heart, with the vineyards now taking centre stage. He is as passionate about vines as his now-retired father was passionate about mixed farming – 'both of them have the "farming bug"', says Pascale. The vines themselves may be relatively young but they are bred to a family tradition of winegrowing that was old long before François Rabelais was born.

Above: Wine label, inspired by the Bonnaventure crest that also features a cluster of grapes. The wine in question is a Chinon AOC red, one of a range of six red wines (all exclusively Cabernet Franc) and two whites (both Chenin, one a Chinon bottling and the other a Touraine). In the 19th century these vineyards were all but wiped out by *Phylloxera Vastatrix*, with only one hectare still in production when Etienne took over in 1988 (which was also the year that he and Pascale got married).

Above: Château de Coulaine: once a 15th-century farm-cum-fortified house, now a gracious country residence in the Gothic Revival style. Featured here, rising regally above four corbelled turrets, is the 15th-century projecting stair tower that looks out over the nearby River Vienne. The ornate stone windows and door frames are 19th century, as is the former orangery (glimpsed far right), now the tasting room.

Left: The south-facing dining room, decorated in the neo-Gothic style dear to Henri Quirit de Coulaine. Walnut table and chairs, oak dresser and fabric wall hanging create a graceful setting for large family reunions 'when everyone lends a hand,' says Pascale, 'regardless of age or sex!'

Opposite, above, left: Tapestry-covered chair on first-floor landing, in the shady blue light of a north-facing window. The upholstery was hand embroidered by Etienne's great-grandmother.

Opposite, above, right: The tasting room (formerly the orangery) is located away from the château itself. Hence this sign, propped against an enormous cedar tree – essential to prevent visitors getting lost.

Opposite, below, left: View from the interior of the wine cellar through a curtain of green ivy.

Opposite, below, right: A child's high chair in the dining room.

Opposite: The 'chambre jaune' (yellow bedroom) on the first floor: one of four *chambres d'hôte*, each with an en-suite bathroom, located in the corbelled turrets. Seen through the pointed-arch door is the single bedroom adjoining the double bedroom in the foreground. The furnishings are a mix of old and new – stripped floorboards, antique chest of drawers, modern finishings.

Left: Portrait in the single bedroom pictured opposite – subject and artist unknown.

Above: A lady's dressing table in the single bedroom.

Opposite: The former *magnanerie* (silk-worm nursery) now houses Etienne and his family. Pictured here is the warm and unpretentious kitchen. The château itself remains home to Etienne's parents, who have lived there since the Second World War; also his two elder sisters, Catherine de Bonnaventure and Isabelle de Kerros.

Above: The table in the centre of the tasting room is made from an unused wooden tank found by Etienne when he was renovating the winery.

Right: Barrels of Coulaine's old-vines *cuvée* – an almost seamless blend of wood and tuffeau. The estate's oldest vines are 50–80 years old, the oldest parcels being *en fermage*.

CHÂTEAU DE TRACY

The records say wine has been produced here since 1396, but the vineyards were probably established long before that – in Gallo-Roman times, if not earlier. In 1586 the estate was acquired through marriage by François d'Estutt d'Assay, a noble of Scottish descent whose forebears – the Stutt family – had rallied to the cause of future French king Charles VII in the Hundred Years War. Rewarded with the fiefdom of d'Assay and French naturalization, they gallicized their name to d'Estutt d'Assay.

Move forward now some 400 years to the 1950s when the late Jacqueline d'Estutt d'Assay, Château de Tracy heiress, marries Count Alain d'Estutt d'Assay (two branches of the same family). It is their son, Count Henry d'Estutt d'Assay, who owns this property today. 'My father raised me to believe that privilege carries responsibility, and that nobility is defined by deeds and not by birthright. My duty, as head of this estate, is to make good wine – and that in turn depends on a happy, motivated workforce and sustainable vineyard practices.'

Henry d'Assay is heir to a long and inspiring legacy. Antoine Louis Claude d'Estutt, Count of Tracy in the 18th century, was a social reformer and disciple of John Locke. The first to coin the term 'ideology', he was a committed abolitionist and friends with General de Lafayette – whose son married the Count's daughter – and also Thomas Jefferson, whose principles he espoused. Jefferson wrote the preface to the Count's 'Treatise on Political Economy', commenting that it would encourage 'a just and regular distribution of the public burdens from which we have sometimes strayed.' Other leading lights in the Count's circle were Benjamin Franklin and George Washington. The Count's son, Victor de Tracy, was among the French deputies who voted for the abolition of slavery. He himself married Sarah Newton, niece of English physicist Isaac Newton, and is remembered as a champion of agronomic reform. In more recent times, Henry's father Count Alain d'Assay made three attempts to escape from German prisoner-of-war camps, shared his meagre rations with younger prisoners and weighed just 43 kilos (barely 100 pounds) on his return home. In fact the only blot on this otherwise immaculate historical landscape is the renegade lord who owned – but then eventually lost – the château in the 14th century. Banished for siding with the English at the start of the Hundred Years War, he was dispossessed of his 'house and heritage' in 1339 (long before the Stutts left Scotland).

The château's present occupants are Henry, his wife Corinne and their two teenage sons. The place they call 'home' is a fairytale château on the eastern bank of the Loire – romantic towers and turrets peeking through densely wooded grounds. Nestled at the foot of the castle is the village of Tracy-sur-Loire, across the river from Sancerre. The vineyards, restored to greatness by Henry's parents, comprise some 30 hectares of Sauvignon Blanc plantings. The soils – Kimmeridgian marls, limestone and flint – are pure Pouilly-Fumé. 'I very much hope that my sons will take over one day,' says their father, 'but only if they feel called to this life – only if they have that vocation.'

The 'grande tour' (great tower) rises majestically from the surrounding landscape, its pointed roofs visible all the way from Sancerre (some five miles to the west, across the river). Château de Tracy dates from the late 14th to early 15th centuries, originally built as a fortress that probably guarded the Loire crossing at this point. The 'grande tour' was one of four corner towers in the fortress walls. Considered 'too claustrophobic' by subsequent owners, two of the walls were demolished in the 19th century. Particular features are the projecting stair tower (centre), fine chimneystack (left of the stair tower) and *bartizans* (overhanging battlement corner turrets).

Above: Practically every century has brought changes to the château. Glimpsed here on the far right is the 15th-century tower (pictured overleaf). The tower immediately to its left dates from the 17th–18th centuries (deduced from its unusually wide staircase). All of the pointed tower roofs date from the 19th century, as do the chimneystacks (left).

Opposite, above, left: Window overlooking inner courtyard, wreathed in wisteria: the château is a showcase for the green-fingered talents of Corinne d'Assay.

Opposite, above, right: An inscription in one of the *bartizans*.

Opposite, below, left: Original nail-studded plank door (15th century) opening into the donjon.

Opposite, below, right: Servants' entrance into tower added in the 19th century, reserved for the use of staff (now long gone) lodged on the second floor.

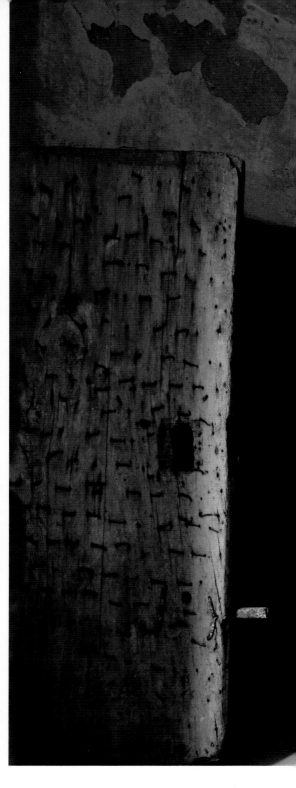

Above: The 'grand salon' on the ground floor. The fireplace is 15th–16th century, the only source of heating in this room. 'Thick walls do all the same keep it remarkably snug, except in the coldest months, at Christmas, for instance, when we have visitors – then we have to burn an entire oak tree for three days just to raise the temperature to 17–18 degrees Celsius,' says Corinne d'Assay. The windows and parquet floor, which would be highly unusual in a fortress, are probably later additions. The decor is 20th century, dating from the days of the late Jacqueline d'Estutt d'Assay.

Above: The first floor of the donjon, with close-up of nail-studded door pictured on the preceding pages. The doors are made with two thicknesses of wood, fastened by wrought-iron nails hammered over for extra strength. The cast-iron fireplace plaque is original and inscribed with the family crest (motto: 'don bien acquis', meaning 'well gotten gain'). Heraldic supporters are a lion or leopard, featured here on the chimneybreast.

CHAMPAGNE

ROEDERER

Chalk is the Champagne region's white gold. Champagne vines thrive in it and bottled Champagne wines age best of all in chalk cellars. Without chalk there would be no Champagne industry and no great Champagne Houses in Reims, once the regional capital and still the Champagne capital of France.

Foremost among the major Champagne Houses is Louis Roederer, whose family residence stands in splendour on the elegant Boulevard Lundy in Reims. It is built on a thick seam of chalk, thick enough for cellar construction, which also attracted Krug and Lanson, rival Champagne Houses. Known as *crayères*, the cellars were originally excavated for building materials, leaving a legacy of cathedral-like galleries that later proved ideal for the maturation of bottled Champagne.

Paris, like Reims, was built on chalk, extracted from below to build above. But in the Middle Ages Reims, the spiritual capital of medieval France, was a thriving city while Paris was still a collection of hovels along the Seine. Its cathedral is one of the oldest in France, site of French coronations for more than 800 years, starting with Clovis in the 5th century and including Joan of Arc's protégé, Charles VII ('Le Dauphin') in 1429.

The Roederer family's connection with Reims goes back to 1776 when the business began life as Dubois Père et Fils. By the time Louis Roederer I, the founding patriarch, died in 1870 Louis Roederer Champagne was number one worldwide. Annual shipments exceeded 2.5 million bottles, of which nearly one third went to Russia. The famous Cuvée Cristal was tailor-made for Tsar Alexander II in 1876. The love affair with Russia ended abruptly in 1917 when the collapse of the Tsarist regime put paid to Roederer's main export market. But within just a few decades the Roederer star was back in the ascendant and the House today is one of the oldest and largest of the independent Champagne producers. 'We got where we are today by staying true to who we are,' says current Managing Director Frédéric Rouzaud. 'I think of us as a small boat that grew into a big ship without ever veering off course.'

The residence stands alongside the Roederer administrative headquarters, built in 1853 with chalk cellars below. The family lived on the top floor until 1927 when an opportunity came to purchase the house next door: the Maison Alfred Werlé, built in the 1860s by the heir to Veuve Clicquot. It was renamed the Hôtel Louis Roederer by Léon Olry-Roederer, Frédéric's great-grandfather.

The building's magnificent sweeping façade is typical of the Louis XVI style. The house was the first of the grand mansions to grace this spacious avenue, setting the style for those that followed. The architect was Reims-born Alphonse Gosset, who also designed one of the city's landmark buildings, the Grand Théâtre de Reims. The house was recently redecorated by Frédéric, whose aim was to 'warm up some of its more grandiose-seeming features, using contemporary materials and furnishings, and to restore natural materials to their original eloquence.' Looking around the house today one senses a family rooted in tradition, but with both feet firmly in the present. In a world where independence is not the norm, the Hôtel Louis Roederer stands as a monument to the enduring strength of family enterprise.

The house was badly damaged in the First World War but has since been scrupulously and faithfully reconstructed. The ground floor was the only part of the building left intact. Pictured here is the magnificent marble staircase in the main entrance hall, still with its original floor. Formerly carpeted, the stairs have been laid bare and the iron handrail has been stripped back to its original dark-metal tones. The furnishings are mid-19th century (like the house itself) and include various treasures purchased by the family over the years – such as the six-panelled Chinese lacquered screen glimpsed on the right.

Opposite and above:
The main reception room, the first in a succession of three rooms, connecting through a smaller reception room to the dining room. Featured here is a portrait of former head of house Louis Roederer II. Beneath it stands a marble-topped oak sideboard, formerly in the pressing centre where it was used to dress game in the hunting season. On the table in the foreground is a register of the vineyards owned by Roederer in 1945.

A smaller reception room is visible through doorways to left and right of the fireplace (above). The portrait, in the background on the right, painted by John Hoppner (1758–1810) shows Queen Louise of Prussia.

Right: Portrait of man reclining, thought to be Louis Roederer I (with faithful hound at his feet).

Left: The small reception room is a perfect example of what Frédéric Rouzaud describes as a 'contemporary take on a traditional setting.' Chandeliers are painted in more modern tones, the lighting is warmer and kinder, and the furniture is more modern, especially the sofas. 'We felt that the materials, old and new alike, had to speak for themselves.'

Opposite: The small reception room opens into the dining room – a space reserved for special family occasions, bathed in light from tall flanking windows or lit by the myriad bulbs of this exuberant crystal chandelier. The décor is refined but delightfully engaging, creating a warm, intimate space reflected in a magnificent 15 ft (4.5 m) high mirror.

Left: The entrance hall of no. 74 rue de Savoie in Reims, location of the Louis Roederer cellars since the late 19th century. Originally constructed by Louis Roederer I, the cellars were rebuilt in the 1930s – still the only example of Art Deco business premises in Reims. 'Bubbles' of natural light are shed by the plaster-and-glass ceiling dome – a frothy fantasy reflected in the mirrors on the left of the picture. The floor slabs are 'pierre de Courville' (from a quarry just outside Reims). The bust in the centre is Cristal patron Russian Tsar Alexander II. Displayed behind him are mechanical relics from former days in Champagne: filter, pump, etc.

Above: A small wooden figurine carved into a baby's crib (now used for floral arrangements) on the ground floor of the Louis Roederer residence.

Right: Antique Champagne riddling rack (*pupitre*) on display in the Louis Roederer cellars. Cristal bottles (because they are flat-bottomed) and non-standard size bottles (such as Jeroboams) are still turned by hand. Two professional *remueurs* (hand riddlers) work at a rate of 51,000 bottles a day. Riddling these days is otherwise computer controlled.

TAITTINGER

'We are men of faith – and generosity,' says Pierre-Emmanuel Taittinger, head of the Taittinger House since 2006. Faith, religious and otherwise, has certainly played a major role in the Taittinger fortunes: its story reads like a celebration of the Divine through human achievement, perfectly epitomized by this gracious 18th-century country house near Epernay. Château de la Marquetterie is where it all started.

The property is tucked into a hillside overlooking the Premier Cru village of Pierry, amid a sea of vines that were first planted by Benedictine monks in the 14th century. The architecture is typical of the French Enlightenment, designed by a nephew of Anges-Jacques Gabriel who was chief architect to Louis XV. Some 200 years after it was built, Château de la Marquetterie would become the cradle of a Champagne House whose origins are inseparable from the history of Champagne itself. 'It would be unthinkable to make wine without this historical dimension,' insists Pierre-Emmanuel. 'For committed Bonapartists like us history is something to be cherished. My son Clovis, for instance, is named after the first king of the Franks.'

Taittinger Champagne was founded by Pierre-Emmanuel's grandfather, Pierre-Charles Taittinger (1887–1965). As a cavalry officer in the First World War, the young Pierre-Charles saw some of the worst fighting on the Western Front – gaining a distinguished military record that would earn him the French Legion of Honour. His only haven from the bloodshed was this house, then the headquarters of his commanding officer, Marshall Joffre. Pierre-Charles vowed then that if he came through the war alive he would buy this château and its 16-hectare vineyard – which he did, in 1932, having previously acquired venerable Champagne House, Forest et Fourneaux. So it was that one of the oldest Champagne Houses morphed into 20th-century newcomer Taittinger Champagne.

It is certainly tempting to say that this was a marriage made in heaven. Between them Château de la Marquetterie and Forest et Fourneaux span more than a thousand years of history. The château looks out over vineyards that can trace their origins back to the Dark Ages. By the 18th century these vines were managed by Benedictine monks who are widely regarded as the fathers of naturally sparkling Champagne wines. Enter local wine merchant, Jacques Fourneaux, founder of a flourishing business that in 1918 purchased the 13th-century palace of the Counts of Champagne in Reims. Going back a few hundred years, the place was the home of balladeer King of Navarre, Thibaud IV, said to have returned from Cyprus in 1240 with the ancestor of today's Chardonnay. In 1952, as a tribute to his memory, Taittinger released their first 100 per cent Chardonnay prestige *cuvée*, Comtes de Champagne Blanc de Blancs.

Château de la Marquetterie has never been the Taittinger family home. 'We deliberately chose not to live here so as to keep all of its magic intact,' says Pierre-Emmanuel. 'It is reserved for special occasions – VIP receptions, family celebrations – and remains as eternally enchanting for us as it is for our visitors.' This house has certainly looked kindly on the Taittinger destinies. As Pierre-Emmanuel proudly points out, theirs is the only major Champagne House that is still run by someone whose name is the name on the bottle.

The house overlooks the western end of the village of Pierry, just south of Epernay. Construction dates from 1734, also the year that saw the foundation of Champagne House Forest et Fourneaux – both being purchased within a year of each other by Pierre Taittinger. In 1984 his son and successor Claude Taittinger reinstated the original slate roof to mark the 250th anniversary of the château.

Above: The oak-panelled dining room where 18th-century French writer and philosopher Jacques Cazotte (1719–92) once entertained his guests. His tenancy ended in 1792 when his monarchist sympathies cost him his head. Two years later his friend and occasional house guest, the satirical poet André Chénier, was beheaded for alleged 'crimes against the state' (no shortage of those in the Reign of Terror).

Right: View from the dining room into the anteroom, looking through to a portrait of Frère Dom Oudart (1654–1742). Cellar-master at the Abbey of Saint-Pierre-aux-Monts de Châlons, Dom Oudart did much to improve the making and bottling of sparkling wine. His counterpart at the nearby Abbey of Saint-Pierre d'Hautvillers was Dom Pérignon, with whom he no doubt consulted.

Opposite, below, left: Embroidered tapestry stool from a suite in an anteroom connecting with the dining room (pictured opposite, above).

Opposite, below, right: Stairs to first floor with golden figurine crouched at the first step.

Left: The main reception room, featuring chandelier and *commode en tombeau* chest of drawers – among the original furnishings and fittings acquired by Pierre Taittinger in 1932.

Opposite, above, left: Detail from tapestry showing Thibaud IV, Count of Champagne, and Blanche de Castille, Queen of France, tasting Chardonnay wine. Thibaud is also credited with introducing the rose to Europe: the Damascina, a red rose from Jordan. The Count of Lancaster, husband of Thibaud's daughter-in-law, adopted it as his family emblem. The House of York chose a white rose and history did the rest.

Opposite, above, right: Gate to Champagne Taittinger in Reims, displaying seal of Thibaud IV, Count of Champagne.

Opposite, below: The Taittinger cellars, with Thibaud's seal in the background, dusted with light from the opening in the vaulting. The cellars are housed in the magnificent 4th-century *crayères* (chalk caves) beneath the Butte Saint Nicaise in Reims.

BOLLINGER

Coco Chanel once said that she only drank Champagne on two occasions: when she was in love and when she wasn't. For Lily Bollinger, the Champagne she first tasted in 1923 on her engagement to Jacques, the third generation Bollinger to run this estate, became an integral part of her life. Interviewed some 40 years later by British tabloid the *Daily Mail*, she famously commented, 'I drink my Champagne when I'm happy, and when I'm sad. Sometimes I drink it when I'm alone. When I have company I consider it obligatory. I trifle with it if I'm not hungry, and drink it when I am. Otherwise I never touch it – unless I'm thirsty.'

Elizabeth Law de Lauriston Boubers (1899–1977), known as Aunt Lily to her family and Mme Jacques to local people and staff, was one of Champagne's best-loved characters. Widowed at the age of 42, she found herself propelled to the head of a Champagne House beleaguered by occupying German forces. During her 30 years at the helm, Lily Bollinger changed the company's fortunes forever. As former Bollinger president and great-great-grandson of the founder, Ghislain de Montgolfier, rightly points out, 'Instead of taking a back seat when Jacques died in 1941, Lily rose splendidly to the occasion. Here was a woman with no business experience whatsoever, a woman on her own who was prepared to travel the world in the aftermath of the war. Lily's greatest legacy was to establish our reputation far and wide, conquering new markets with her charm, flawless tasting abilities and abundant personality. She also redefined our values, establishing ethical and quality standards that remain our guiding principles today.'

Pictured here behind a sea of casks is the house that was Lily's home for more than 50 years: number 16 rue Jules Lobet in Aÿ, forever known as 'La Maison de Mme Bollinger'. Originally there was just the main building, purchased by the Hennequin de Villermont family in around 1758. This courtyard along with adjoining wings came later, housing the winery proper until 1936 when Bollinger moved production facilities and offices to new premises in the north of Aÿ. The workforce today numbers some 130 employees, unusually large for a Champagne House, but reflecting Bollinger's attachment to traditional techniques. All of its rosé and vintage wines, for example, are hand-riddled and manually disgorged.

One of the great Champagne Houses, Bollinger is rightly praised for its unerring ability to walk the tightrope between tradition and innovation. Practically a household name, Bollinger has thrived on popularization without ever losing its crown. The Champagne preferred by James Bond and the anti-heroines of the British sitcom *Ab Fab* has also enjoyed the royal patronage of six British monarchs, from Queen Victoria to Queen Elizabeth II. King Edward VII was especially fond of Bollinger and, when out shooting, would always be accompanied by a boy wheeling Champagne on ice in a wheelbarrow – hence the expression 'a bottle of the boy' and by extension the nickname 'Bolly'. Bollinger RD ('récemment dégorgé' or 'late disgorged') was served at Prince Charles' bachelor party to celebrate his forthcoming marriage to Diana; and the newly weds toasted their union with Bollinger RD, Vintage 1973. Brut ahead of its time and impeccably understated, Bollinger Champagne has always struck a particular chord with the notoriously reticent British.

Oak casks drying in the sun in the courtyard of number 16 rue Jules Lobet. Originally called the rue de l'Huilerie ('Oil Mill' Road), the street was renamed in the 20th century after a local worthy who started out as a mechanic and panel beater and finished as town councillor and deputy of the Marne region. This courtyard is in front of the house (street frontage is at the rear). Bollinger owns 3,000 casks like these, for vinification of each season's musts.

Left: Portrait of Louise-Charlotte Hennequin de Villermont, daughter of Admiral Count Athanase de Villermont. In 1829 her father joined forces with German-born Joseph-Jacques Bollinger and his associate, Champagne native Paul Renaudin. Together they founded Champagne Renaudin-Bollinger & Cie, with the Villermont family home (i.e., this house) as company head office. Joseph-Jacques Bollinger later married Louise-Charlotte, took French nationality (changing his name to Jacques) and in 1854, with Renaudin and the Admiral now dead, set up his own business. Bollinger Champagne has remained committed to independent family ownership ever since.

Opposite: The entrance hall displays a stylish but artless combination of wood, stone and colourful fabrics, true to the spirit of a house that is nowhere grandiose.

Opposite: The small sitting room, featuring Louis XV *commode en tombeau* chest of drawers with marble top. The overall impression – the bust, the pretty table lamp, the dark blue of the tapestry and the pink of the chair – is unmistakably feminine. One senses that Lily Bollinger would have liked this room.

Above: The sitting room cum library, featuring the bookcases made by Bollinger coopers in the dark days of the 1930s. Bollinger is one of the very few Champagne Houses that still employs a full-time cooper: all of its musts are fermented in oak casks, with small oak barrels for all of its reserve and vintage wines. Reserve wines, unusually, are kept in magnums.

Right: Under the Occupation Lily would patrol her vineyards on a bicycle. Local people knew her as Mme Jacques – the indomitable lady who slept in the cellars after the Germans commandeered the family château. For Lily's great-nephew and former Bollinger president, Arnould d'Hautefeuille, Lily was 'a consummate businesswoman but her greatest pleasure was giving pleasure to others. For us children, Sunday tea time with Tante Lily was always a treat.'

ALSACE

DOMAINE SCHLUMBERGER

'School friends thought we lived in a château, but actually the house was in ruins. The only heated rooms were the bathroom and the nursery. You could see daylight through the roof and we had bats flying round our heads at night,' explains Séverine Schlumberger. The authorities did their best to evict the family, but Eric, Séverine's father, stood his ground. In 1997 the bulldozers moved in and four years later a triumphant Eric Beydon-Schlumberger won his fight to rebuild. Sometimes it makes more sense to knock down and rebuild than to renovate.

Guebwiller, at the southern tip of Alsace, has been the ancestral home of the Schlumberger family since the early 1800s. Alsace has swapped back and forth between French and German rule six times in the past 300 years, but has remained French since the end of the Second World War. The German influence, however, is everywhere – in the architecture, the place names and, of course, the wine.

The new house stands in the centre of Guebwiller, rebuilt from scratch on the site of the former tavern where textile machinery manufacturer Nicolas Schlumberger set up business in 1810. He also established roots in the area, purchasing 20 hectares of vines on the steep hillsides around Guebwiller. But the bulk of the vineyard was pieced together in the early 20th century by Séverine's great-grandfather Ernest Schlumberger, from some 2,500 plots abandoned by their owners following the *Phylloxera Vastatrix* epidemic. As a result, Schlumberger today is one of the very few domaines in France with more than 100 hectares of prime vineyard land, boasting substantial holdings in each of the four local Grand Crus (Kessler, Kitterlé, Searing and Spiegel). The vineyards, pictured here in all their splendour, are some of the most spectacular in Alsace, a fitting tribute to a man who not only rebuilt the estate but also revived the town of Guebwiller itself.

Eric Beydon-Schlumberger, Ernest's grandson, ran this estate for 30 years, establishing a reputation that is upheld today by his daughter Séverine and her uncle Alain, supported by new winemaker Alain Freyburger. More than half of the vineyard is now worked in line with organic or biodynamic methods, and the winery is at the top of its game. But the overriding objective remains forever the same: to make wines that express and respect their *terroir*.

It is the marriage of tradition and creative thinking that defines the Schlumberger estate. We see it in the newly built family home, in vineyard terraces tilled by horse-drawn ploughs – because at these altitudes this is still the most efficient method – and in hundred-year-old oak casks equipped with temperature-control mechanisms that allow slow and careful aging. The rewards are commensurate with the effort: Schlumberger wines, once tasted, are never forgotten. As Séverine says, 'when we make converts, we make them for life.'

Opposite: Rows of vines wrap around the mountains like swaddling bands, hugging 50-degree slopes at altitudes of 750–840 ft (230–250 m). Breaking with convention, the rows follow the contours of the slopes, a practice known as 'horizontal planting' pioneered by Ernest Schlumberger to combat erosion in this steep, sandy terrain. There are some 30 miles of dry-stone terrace walls on these hills – more than twice the quantity of stone used to build Strasbourg Cathedral.

Below: The Schlumberger family home – a faithful reconstruction of a traditional Alsace house, rebuilt in the period from 2004 to 2007. A paint-finished render (in this case, off-white/yellow) is characteristic of the region and actively encouraged by the authorities.

Left: Hanging plants, white walls and a subtle interplay of natural wood finishes creates a thoroughly contemporary ambience, in pleasing contrast to the gothic spires of the 12th-century church of Saint Léger for which Guebwiller is famous. The ground floor opens onto the garden, with huge floor-to-ceiling windows that merge the house with its grounds. The fact that the house was rebuilt from scratch is a statement in itself. 'Innovation for conservation' is a fair summary of the Schlumberger approach.

Opposite: Inside the house, an eclectic mix of the old and the new creates an atmosphere of gracious living. Designer-chic meets up-market comforts, helped by good light and a feeling of spaciousness.

DOMAINE WEINBACH

In a world that remains a predominantly male preserve, unusually the owners of this estate are women. Their mere presence, of course, would have been unthinkable in pre-Revolutionary France when monasteries were strictly off limits to women. In his account of a visit to the Capuchin Friars Minor in 1676 an anonymous author wrote that he and his family 'couldn't actually enter the building because there were women with us.' Three centuries later the estate founded by those same friars in 1612 is entirely in the hands of women: Colette Faller and her two daughters, Catherine and Laurence.

This property has been their family home since 1898, rebuilt on the site of a Franciscan monastery consecrated in 1619. It stands on the outskirts of the idyllic village of Kaysersberg, birthplace in 1875 of world-famous philanthropist and humanitarian Albert Schweitzer. Laurence Faller today maintains a tradition of winemaking that dates back to the Roman period, the latest in a long line of talented winemakers to emerge from the ever vine-friendly soils of the Kaysersberg Valley.

Few winegrowers are more irrevocably linked to their *terroir* than this formidable trio of Alsatian women. 'When it comes to diversity, we are particularly fortunate,' says Laurence, 'even in a region as renowned for its varied geology as Alsace. It is this diversity that allows us to produce so many different styles of wine.' Weinbach offerings range from bone-dry to lusciously sweet, but all have that good balancing acidity that makes Alsace wines natural companions to food. 'Our sweet wines are delicious with spicy, oriental cuisine, while our dry wines slip down a treat with Thai fish-based dishes,' says Laurence. The elegant Weinbach Cuvée Sainte Catherine, for instance, was the perfect match for the *mousseline de grenouilles* (frog mousse) created by the late Paul Haeberlin, chef-patron of the celebrated Michelin three-starred restaurant l'Auberge de l'Ill near Colmar.

Frogs are increasingly rare in Alsace these days, but snails continue to be a major feature of local fare. The high point of Weinbach's centenary celebrations in 1998 was a snail banquet in memory of the Capuchin friars who gave their name to the walled vineyard surrounding the property: the Clos des Capucins, now the emblem of Domaine Weinbach. 'Wine', says Laurence, 'has a life of its own. There is a mystic side to wine that cannot be fully explained, one that requires great sensitivity on the part of the winegrower. Our approach is based on minimum intervention, adapting as necessary to the needs of our vines and their environment, remembering always that good wine begins with good grapes.'

Total plantings today comprise some 28 hectares of biodynamically grown vineyards, mainly located in the commune of Kaysersberg. The grapes are harvested manually by a faithful team of pickers who return every year. Lunch time finds them gathered in the kitchen back at the house, seated around a solid wood table with space for 40 guests.

Colette Faller picked up the baton when husband Théo died in 1979. She and her eldest daughter Catherine now handle sales and marketing, while Laurence is in charge of the vineyards and winemaking. Domaine Weinbach today is a flourishing success, fêted by critics worldwide for its exacting quality standards.

Opposite: The Clos des Capucins, with the L-shaped house in the background. The vineyard was created to the greater glory of God in nature, by Capuchin friars whose inspiration was Saint Francis of Assisi. The house itself was acquired by brothers Théodore and Jean-Baptiste Faller in 1898. Tanners by trade, the Faller brothers divided their time between their tanning factory in Kaysersberg and their vineyard at the Clos des Capucins. Essential to both of these activities is water – hence the importance of the River Weiss (running through Kaysersberg) and the Weinbach stream (flowing past the Domaine).

Left: The main entrance to the property, in the wall surrounding the Clos, thought to date from the 1800s. The house and vineyards are located on south-facing slopes.

Opposite, above, left: Théodore Faller was an avid collector of antiques. One example is this lovely wood-cased clock with a delicate vine motif inlay.

Opposite, above, right: Katy Faller, pictured here in the 1960s with her great-aunt.

Opposite, below: The smaller of the two reception rooms. The furnishings are 19th century, but with a clean, contemporary finish that is quite literally 'embodied' in the striking bronze torso with blue patina displayed on the desk. The sculptor is an old school friend of Laurence Faller – a teacher by profession she says, but a true artist at heart.

Above: The main reception room is characteristic of this property, which is 'family home' first and 'château' second. The carpet's pink and silver floral motif finds an offbeat echo in the electric rainbow stripes of the sofa and the feather-like whiteness of the glass chandelier. This touch of lightness and frivolity sits well with the sober expressions of times past that surround it: wood-panelled walls hung with fading family photographs; dark, heavy bookcase displaying antique memorabilia.

Left: The wine storehouse, located in the semi-basement beneath the short wing of the house, in the chapel of the former monastery. A cross inscribed over a now-sealed doorway marks the original entrance. The high water table made the construction of cellars impossible – hence the semi-basement. The larger vats (right) have a capacity of 40hl. Those beyond hold 30hl.

Above: The big, warm kitchen at Domaine Weinbach, featuring the huge table where Laurence's small son, Armand, once dozed as a baby in his canvas chair, lulled by the gentle simmering of cooking pans and the soporific fumes of crystalline wines.

Right: Old bottles of wine with faded labels ... a sight to delight the eye of any wine lover. These are bottles given in exchange for Weinbach bottlings – Alsace Rieslings swapped for ... ah, but that would be telling.

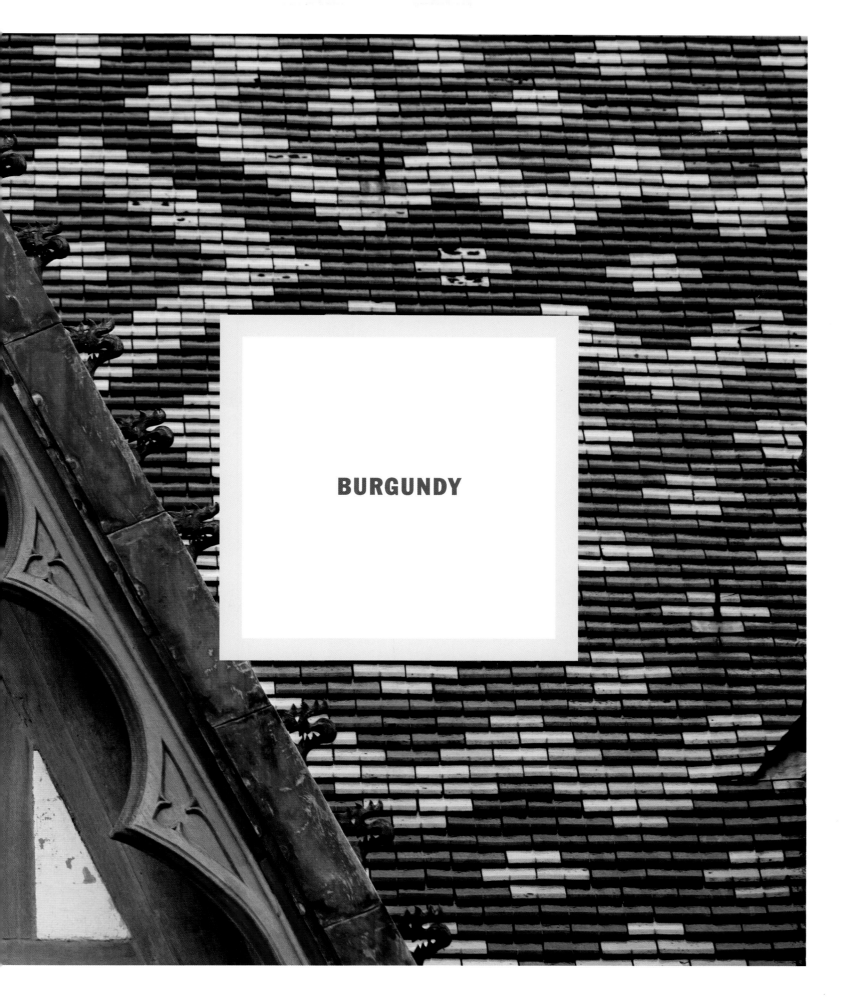

BURGUNDY

CHÂTEAU DE CHOREY-LES-BEAUNE

It would be hard to imagine a more authentically Burgundian estate than this one, namesake of the village of Chorey-les-Beaune. *Les* denotes near: Beaune, capital of the Burgundy wine region, is just over a mile away. This is the heart of the historic Côte d'Or, comprising the Côte de Nuits in the north (fabulous red wines) and the Côte de Beaune in the south (fabulous red and white wines). The name Côte d'Or is an abbreviation of Côte d'Orient, meaning 'eastern slope', a reference to the prime, southeast-facing aspect of its finest vineyards. Plumb in the middle sits Château de Chorey-les-Beaune, 'less than an hour from everything there is to see,' says owner François Germain. And he should know. A Burgundian born and bred, he has lived in this château since early childhood, heir to an estate that was founded in 1908 by his great-grandfather, Pierre Germain. Now with 11 grandchildren of his own, François leaves the winemaking to son Benoît while he builds up the family's *chambres d'hôte* business. 'Two closely linked activities, with wine at their heart,' he says. François' home-made jams provide a strong incentive to sample Benoît's handiwork, by staying at the château...

A visit to Château de Chorey must surely rank as one of the high points of a trip to Burgundy (even in a region with such a wealth of attractions as this). The property dates from the 13th century, founded on the site of a former Merovingian cemetery. The original construction was a moated, fortified manor house where villagers would take refuge in times of trouble – essential in an era when peace was the exception. The Hundred Years War (1337–1453) left most of the castle in ruins, except for the moat and towers. The other buildings date from the 17th and 18th centuries, including a typically Burgundian 17th-century dovecote with

Above, left: The front of the house, looking out over 2.5 hectares of vineyards that surround the château. Total holdings run to 17 hectares, scattered (as is traditional in Burgundy) across a variety of Premier Crus vineyards. Plantings are predominantly Pinot Noir, with small blocks of Chardonnay.

Above, right: The tower in the foreground dates from the 13th century, while the dovecote just visible behind it was built in the 17th century. On the right you see the back of the house, with tower attached.

1,700 nesting boxes (*boulins*) and an impressive spiral staircase. In France the right to own a dovecote remained a noble prerogative until the Revolution when it was promptly abolished – presumably, quips François, because what the pigeons fed off was the peasants' corn seed. The *colombine* – pigeon droppings – was a much-prized fertilizer and formed part of every well-born bride's dowry.

'In Burgundy, people make their own wines, grow their own grapes and manage their own vineyards,' declares François with pride. All of their vines are now organically grown, Benoît firmly believing that great wine begins in the vineyard. His father is a champion of all things Burgundian and most especially the Pinot Noir. 'When locally grown, the Pinot Noir is the best grape in the world,' says François. 'And the most difficult to replicate elsewhere.' To make his point, three of the château's five guest rooms are named after the family's Beaune Premier Cru holdings: Les Vignes Franches, Les Teurons and Les Cras. Each room features a double, four-poster bed, and is decorated to match – a standard of accommodation that has earned the château a four *épis* rating. The château, like the Pinot Noir, boasts impeccable credentials. This is the Côte d'Or, famous for its clay limestone soils, its intricate patchwork of vineyards and magnificent wines. In such a place only the best will do and no one knows that better than François Germain.

Above, left: Reflections of the house in the still waters of the moat that meanders gracefully at the foot of its walls. Just visible on the right is an ancient cedar tree, one of several very fine specimens that grace these elegant grounds.

Above, right: A wrought-iron gate, dating from 1608, separates house and vineyard. The house was rebuilt in the 17th century by the Migieu family, owners of Château de Savigny-lès-Beaune. At that time it served as their farmhouse and only the first floor was living quarters, reserved for the *régisseur* (estate manager).

Opposite: Double doors in the dining room lead to the sitting room. The doors were added some 100 years ago by François' great-grandfather, Pierre Germain, as part of a general programme of refurbishment.

Right: The kitchen, entered from the opposite end of the dining room through double doors in the same style as those that lead to the sitting room. The floor was part of Pierre Germain's refurbishments, while the plasterwork and friezes were recently renovated by François. Note the ancient spit-roasting mechanism to the right of the fireplace. Displayed on the chimneybreast are family hunting trophies, large and small.

Opposite, above:
A handsomely carved oak door gives access to the staircase from the landing. Pierre Germain's initials are displayed above the carved motif.

Opposite, below, left:
Portrait of François' great-aunt Tante Berthe, Mother Superior of Les Sœurs Hospitalières de l'Hôtel-Dieu in Beaune. It was she who prevented her brother, Paul Germain (François' grandfather), from selling the estate in the aftermath of the Great Depression. Some ten years ago, François honoured her contribution with a *cuvée* in her name – Tante Berthe (1999).

Right: The three bedrooms on the first floor are each named after the estate's Premier Cru holdings – this one is called Les Vignes Franches. All five guest rooms have bathrooms en suite.

Left: Attention to fine detail is everywhere you look, making every room feel warm and inviting. The house can accommodate up to 15 guests at a time, with spacious family suites on the ground floor.

Opposite: The Les Teurons bedroom, with grand canopied bed for two, and traditional *lit bateau* for one. The bearded gentleman in the portrait on the wall is Pierre Germain.

Overleaf: The village of Pernand-Vergelesses, on the western side of the hill of Corton, at the northern tip of the Côte de Beaune. Here and throughout Burgundy plantings are dominated by the Pinot Noir (for red wines), supported by the Chardonnay (for white wines). Watching over the village, crowning the wooded peak in the background, is the monument of Notre-Dame de Bonne-Espérance. Just over a mile to the southeast lies the village of Chorey-les-Beaune and its eponymous château.

CHÂTEAU DE BÉRU

The Chablis wine area lies at the northernmost tip of Burgundy, a full hundred miles closer to Paris than the Côte d'Or. Just 37 miles to the south of Champagne, the region is notorious for its cold winters and damp weather conditions. 'In 2007 hail stones the size of golf balls wiped out 80 per cent of our grape crop in a single storm,' recalls Athénaïs de Béru. Weather conditions apart, she is blessed with an enviable birthright. Château de Béru, family seat of the Counts of Béru since 1620, is the most impressive address in the village: a classified monument, medieval in origin, surrounded by the only walled vineyard in the whole of Chablis. The property was founded in the 13th century, then enlarged and rebuilt during the Renaissance and again in the 18th century. The eastern gateway, facing the village, features a 15th-century moondial – one of only two in Europe and the only one still in use. Scientists come to take readings every year, checking for the least sign of disruption in the lunar cycle. 'Proving', says Athénaïs, 'that the lunar influence is real. A winemaker knows that working in harmony with the phases of the moon does bring results.'

It says something about the success of her methods that all of Château de Béru's wines are now organically produced from organically grown fruit. Particularly when you consider that there was nothing left of these vineyards just 25 years ago. Ravaged by *Phylloxera Vastatrix* in the late 19th century like every other vineyard in France and in Europe, they were replanted nearly a century later by Count Eric de Béru. 'My father's background was in import–export,' explains Athénaïs. 'But his real passion lay here – in these vineyards that he replanted in 1987. The château then was my grandparents' home – the place where my father grew up and later spent most weekends and holidays, wife and children in tow.' She remembers, in particular, how surprised and delighted he was at her own venture into winemaking. 'By 2002 I realized I had missed my true vocation, so I dropped my City career and signed up for an oenology diploma in Beaune.' Her first vintage was the Clos Béru 2005, released shortly before her father's tragic demise in 2006. 'He always left us free to choose our own careers – but from the moment I came on board, he taught me everything he knew.'

The estate – vineyards, reception facilities and *chambres d'hôte* – is now entirely managed by Athénaïs and her mother Laurence, the Count's widow. 'You have to be a one-man band in this business,' says Athénaïs. 'Burgundy winegrowers make and market their own wines, knowing that every vintage is only as expressive as the *terroir* that produced it in that particular year. The Clos Béru 2009 is the wine from the Clos Béru in 2009 – no more, no less. Pure Chardonnay, from a single named vineyard.' Unlike Bordeaux, Burgundy wines are never blended: the reds are made with Pinot Noir and the whites with Chardonnay. You could say that this château expresses that same uncompromising identity: unspoilt, unadulterated and admirably true to its roots.

Above: The façade of the house on the courtyard entrance side, with the sundial in view. On the other side facing onto the village is a 15th-century moondial – one of only two in Europe. The other one, no longer in use, is at Queens' College, Cambridge.

Above: Back view of the house, looking out over five hectares of Chardonnay plantings on the southern slope of the Béru Valley. Known as the Clos Béru, the vineyard is enclosed by a 13th-century wall. Total holdings amount to some 15 hectares – all Chardonnay – located around the village itself.

Right: Renaissance archway under the south wing, leading to a lawned garden with pool. Beyond is a square gateway that looks out onto the Clos Béru. The house and grounds are open to the public, but remain the private home of Laurence de Béru, Athénaïs' mother.

Opposite: The main entrance hall runs the length of the ground floor and gives onto the main reception rooms. It is unusually light for a hallway, thanks to windows at the front and back of the house. The square Art Deco chandelier is the work of French master glazier Louis Barillet, designer of the stained glass windows in Chartres Cathedral, working with the French architect Robert Mallet-Stevens. Against the wall is a Gothic wedding chest, overlooked by various hunting trophies (some of them bagged by present chatelaine Laurence de Béru). The black-and-white tiled floor dates from the 18th century.

Right: An eclectic but tasteful collection of paintings and furnishings gives the hallway a very warm and welcoming feel. A gilt-framed portrait of a sober young lady sits well with the muted tones of the floral wallpaper.

Below, left: Assorted walking sticks and handmade canes used by various ancestors.

Below, right: Eighteenth-century fabric-covered screen displaying perspective paintings.

Above: Drawing room off the hallway, furnished in the Louis XVI style, with antiques and bibelots from all over Europe. The Renaissance table in the middle of the room is Florentine.

Left: A small triptych of Madonna and Child, possibly Italian. The crystal *dragée* dishes in the foreground are of Irish origin.

Opposite: Wood-panelled 'blue' reception room across the hallway from the drawing room featured above. The young man in the painting on the left was named Edmé – a tradition in the de Béru family. Athénaïs' 25-year-old brother is the latest in a long line of Béru males to bear the name.

Left: Reception and tasting room for group functions and paying guests, in the converted stables (east wing). The building dates from the Renaissance and retains many original features such as the stone walls with built-in horse troughs.

Opposite: The oak-panelled dining room in the main house (alongside the 'blue' room), hung with portraits of King Louis XIV and Athénaïs de Montespan, namesake of the present Athénaïs, and Louis' favourite mistress.

CHÂTEAU FUISSÉ

The Pouilly-Fuissé appellation, in the heart of Burgundy's famed Mâconnais region, encompasses some of the most celebrated Chardonnay vineyards in France. Foremost among the region's wineries is Château Fuissé, ancestral seat of the Vincent family since 1862 when the estate was acquired by Claude Bulland. It was his son-in-law, Jacques Vincent, who helped to found the Pouilly-Fuissé appellation. One of his forebears once rode into battle wearing the suit of armour that now stands in the immense great hall. It was christened 'Archibalde' by Jacques' four great-grandchildren, including Bénédicte and Antoine, who now run the estate. 'Today the great hall serves as the wine-tasting room,' explains Bénédicte, 'but for me it will always remain the "grande salle", a place rich with memories of childhood. Huge family gatherings around the immense table, winter evenings by the massive fireplace, snow-blanketed vineyards framed in the tall windows.'

Pouilly-Fuissé is one of the two jewels in the crown of the Mâconnais region: Saint Véran is the other. This estate boasts holdings in both. With an enviable 25 hectares in Pouilly-Fuissé and seven in Saint Véran, Château Fuissé is one of the largest family-owned and -operated wineries in Burgundy. It is also one of the few Burgundy producers to have resisted the fragmentation that is commonly caused by French inheritance laws: the average Pouilly-Fuissé holding rarely exceeds ten hectares. 'We have always sought to keep the estate in one piece,' says Bénédicte. 'This house is, in a way, what holds it all together, symbolizing our belief in the defining role of *terroir*. There are varietal-driven wines and there are *terroir*-driven wines – our wines, exclusively based on the Chardonnay, fall into the latter category. Nowhere in France is the concept of *terroir* more fondly embraced than in Burgundy.'

The house and grounds are inseparable and the relationship between them is sacrosanct. This château, with its adjoining *clos* (an ancient walled vineyard), is the perfect illustration. The property stands on the northern border of Beaujolais and represents a mixture of styles. The main building dates from the 15th century and boasts an unusual pentagonal tower with arrow slits in the walls. Along with the imposing doorway, this suggests that the building was originally a fortified farmhouse. The overhanging roof with its red, curved tiles is typical of the Burgundian Romanesque style – a reminder that the population of this area grew up around the powerful Benedictine abbey of Cluny. The Renaissance porch displays the date 1604 and the cellars were added in the 17th century – built at ground level to avoid disturbing the natural springs beneath the property. 'The cellars are my other favourite place,' says Bénédicte. 'I love their huge beams and rows of fat-bellied barrels. This is where our flagship wines see wood – Le Clos, Les Combettes and Les Brûlés, all Vincent monopoly holdings that we are grooming for promotion to Premier Cru status.'

To have survived and prospered for nearly 200 years in the fiercely competitive Burgundy market is no mean feat. The winery today consists of more than 30 hectares complemented since 1985 by its *négociant* label, 'Jean-Jacques Vincent et Fils'. Bénédicte and Antoine are the fifth generation of the family to steer this ship. Bénédicte handles public relations, her oenologist brother Antoine makes the wines, and her husband, Philippe Tuimder, sells them. Their father, Jean-Jacques Vincent, also a qualified oenologist, is the *éminence grise* behind the operation. In 2003 he passed the baton to his son and daughter, surprised and delighted that they should prove such willing successors.

Château Fuissé, with fine view of the 15th-century pentagonal tower and flanking yew trees. Pictured below are two examples of antique memorabilia collected by co-founder of the Pouilly-Fuissé appellation, Jacques Vincent, great-grandfather of the present owners.

Above, left: Wrought iron lantern, mounted on a wall bracket, in the Renaissance porch in the perimeter wall. In the centre of the bracket is the family coat of arms, flanked by the words 'Château Fuissé, haut lieu de Bourgogne' (Château Fuissé, high-spot of Burgundy).

Above, right: Reproduction of a medieval tapestry with a winemaking theme, on display in the great hall. This part of the house, like the cellars, dates from the 17th century.

Right: The monumental fireplace in the great hall, surrounded by antiques and winemaking memorabilia collected over a lifetime by Jacques Vincent, great-grandfather of Bénédicte and her brother Antoine who run the estate today.

Opposite: A *table à pétrain* (bakery table) in the small tasting room at the entrance to the cellars. At the end of the room stands a wooden statuette of Saint Vincent, patron saint of vignerons.

CHÂTEAU DES PÉTHIÈRES

Château des Péthières is the property of Guy Brac de la Perrière, who now lives here full time since selling up his vineyards in New Zealand. 'It was a perfect fit, really – harvesting in New Zealand in the spring and here in the fall.' 'Here' is a gracious country estate, set in the granite hills of northern Beaujolais. Just five miles to the north is the family's seigneurial seat of Château de la Perrière, jewel in the crown of a rich portfolio of holdings that have survived France's tumultuous history. Quite an achievement, considering that at least five of Guy's forbears lost their heads in the French Revolution. They include Jacques Joseph Brac de la Perrière who in 1794 had the dubious privilege of sharing the same tumbrel as prominent nobleman and scientist Antoine-Laurent de Lavoisier – now remembered as the father of modern chemistry. 'Fortunately for all concerned, Jacques Joseph left 11 children – a prolific breeder like the rest of us.' Guy himself is one of four brothers, with four children of his own. Brac de la Perrière is one of the oldest (and largest) of the Beaujolais dynasties. This house, originally purchased by Guy's uncle in the 1920s, is a relative newcomer to the family holdings.

The Beaujolais region begins some six miles south of Mâcon, on the southern border of Burgundy. Proximity aside, however, the two regions are quite distinct, and so too are the wines. The climate in Beaujolais is warmer and sunnier – 'the clouds stop at Mâcon', says Guy. The land is more undulating and the only vine in sight is the Gamay Noir à Jus Blanc. The Gamay is to Beaujolais what the Pinot Noir is to Burgundy: an ideal match. And it's all thanks to a particular vinification technique known as 'semi maceration'. The process hinges on the use of whole, uncrushed grapes, which are fermented (with their stalks) in small closed vats. By law, all Beaujolais grapes must be picked by hand. At the end of the harvest the pickers elect the 'harvest queen' – the prettiest girl, who gets to toss a posy of flowers into the vat. 'She herself usually follows shortly afterwards!' laughs Guy. The pickers are mostly students, all carefully vetted by Guy's youngest son, Christian – an engineer by profession but, like his father, definitely a winemaker at heart. The vineyard covers just two hectares, planted to old Gamay vines that produce Beaujolais Nouveau – bottled and released within a few weeks of harvesting – and Beaujolais-not-so-Nouveau – the same *cuvée*, but bottled and released the following spring. The flagship bottling is the 'Château des Péthières Brouilly', sourced from Guy's two-hectare slice of the Château de la Perrière vineyards (15 hectares of plantings in the much-prized Brouilly Cru).

Opposite, above: The front of the house faces north, overlooking the terrace and sunken lawn, with leafy chestnut tree in the foreground. The vineyards occupy the slopes at the back of the house. Built in the early 1800s, the house dates from a time when a suntan was for peasants and only white skin was noble – hence its northern aspect, away from the ardours of the sun.

Opposite, below, left: The winemaking 'log sheet', written in chalk around the vat door. The estate wines are made from 100% Gamay, with no chaptalization (the addition of sugar to beef up the alcohol content).

Opposite, below, right: Château des Péthières Brouilly (red-foil capsules) and Beaujolais (white-foil capsules), with roses in the background (traditionally planted in vineyards to provide early warning of infection, particularly oidium, which shows up first on roses).

Overleaf: The main entrance (26 ft, 8 m wide), featuring an Imperial staircase with divided flights.

Opposite: Wellington boots in the hallway, for pickers who forget to bring their own. Lunch and dinner are also provided throughout the harvest – that's 28 extra mouths to feed every day for at least ten days. The furnishings – here and throughout the house – are French Directoire style (late 18th century).

Above: The immense dining room (50 sq m, 536 sq ft), with space enough for a billiard table too.

Right: Antique silver *tastevin* (winemaker's tasting cup), a gift from Guy's father when his son took over the estate – one of a large collection on display at the château.

JURA

CHÂTEAU D'ARLAY

'Seeing is believing,' says Alain de Laguiche. 'What people realize when they visit d'Arlay is that a property this fine is bound to produce fine wines.' His ancestor Prince Pierre d'Arenberg would be delighted to hear it. The Prince spent ten years and most of his fortune restoring the estate in the early 19th century. At a time when every self-respecting noble had many places of residence, the Prince famously declared that Château d'Arlay was 'more than enough for any man'. He inherited the property in 1823, some 30 years after his grandmother the Comtesse de Lauraguais was guillotined for 'conspiring against the Republic'. It was she who built the house and grounds as they stand today, on the site of a former Minim Monastery. Alain de Laguiche describes her as a 'woman of strict principles but hugely generous with it – had they not chopped off her head, she would probably be remembered as a philanthropist.' Her offence was to refuse a job to a defrocked priest who later became president of a revolutionary tribunal and took his revenge in the form of her head. He himself lost his own shortly afterwards.

Château d'Arlay, deep in the heart of the Jura, lies roughly midway between Beaune in Burgundy and the Swiss border. The vineyard dates back to medieval times, planted on south-facing slopes in the lee of a cone-shaped hill. At the top are the ruins of a 9th-century fortress that was for 250 years a strategic stronghold of the Counts of Chalon-Arlay (aka Princes of Orange), until it was demolished by Louis XI in 1479. In the centuries that followed, the d'Arlay vineyards were claimed for the Spanish then the English crowns, finally reverting to France during the reign of Louis XIV. It was his successor, Louis XV, who restored the lands to their rightful owners – and their descendants still own them today. In the 1960s Alain's father, Count Renaud de Laguiche, took the helm of an estate that had never been sold since its foundation in the 13th century. Wars, French Revolution and decapitations notwithstanding, there has never been a time when these vineyards did not produce wine. Château d'Arlay is the oldest wine-producing château in France – 'a historic monument in the real sense of the word,' says Alain. His mother still lives in the château but Alain manages the estate – house, grounds and 30 hectare vineyard – all in all, a formidable undertaking, comparable to running a village. His father put d'Arlay on the world wine map and for the past 30 years Alain has made sure it has stayed there. Château d'Arlay has and always will be a birthright worth defending.

Below, left: Two suits of armour, from the period 1530–40, once belonging to Philibert de Chalon-Arlay whose nephew René Nassau was his chosen heir. The house was emptied during the Revolution and entirely refurnished by Prince Pierre d'Arenberg who restored his ancestors' armour to its rightful place.

Above: The house's northern aspect is typical of former monastic buildings (which faced north for reasons of austerity). To the right is the western pavilion, one of a matching pair of buildings on either side of the house, originally built by the countess as stables.

Right: The central wing of the château opens at the back onto a cobbled courtyard (its edges just visible here), flanked by wings to either side (formerly the two wings of the monastery). The French windows offer a view through to the grounds beyond.

Opposite: This chess game ('a passion of mine,' says Alain de Laguiche) is displayed on the extreme right of the salon (just visible above, far right).

Above: The 'grand salon' (main reception room), floored with contrasting light- and dark-oak boards in a chevron pattern that radiates from the centre point of the room (directly under the oil chandelier, above, right). The ground-floor furnishings are Bourbon Restoration (Charles X), unchanged since Prince Pierre d'Arenberg's exhaustive renovations (inventories and receipts have been kept to this day). His tastes in design create a remarkably contemporary feel, prefiguring the 'form follows function' credo of 1930s Modernism: chairs and well-upholstered sofas that offer proper support for the back; curving lines that recall the curves of human bodies.

Right: The mouldings around the mirror are thought to date from the 18th century, added by the Comtesse de Lauraguais who is pictured here in a 'flattering' portrait by an unsigned artist.

Left: The fabulous U-shaped library. The first and third cabinets are *trompe-l'œils*, stacked with amusing, anti-revolutionary book titles – Pierre d'Arenberg's revenge for his grandmother's beheading. The first cabinet also conceals the chimney conduit for the porcelain stove in the centre of the room (bottom right). The mahogany stepladder, with handrails shaped like elephant trunks, is 18th-century Parisian.

Above: D'Arlay Pinot Noir 1929 vintage (for display only). Vin Jaune, on the other hand, will keep for 50 to 100 years or more. The wine is unique to the Jura and exclusively bottled in 62 cl (21 oz) 'clavelins' (pictured here).

SAVOIE

DOMAINE DE MÉJANE

Domaine de Méjane is not an ancestral family property. It was purchased by
Jean Henriquet in 1995. 'Love at first sight,' he says. Even the name is new,
picked by Jean shortly after he bought the house. The story of this estate,
heroically revived after 50 years of neglect, is all the same a victory for a
traditional way of life that is fast disappearing in Savoie. 'In the 1950s,' says
Jean, 'there were at least 40 winegrowers in this village. Today there are just
four.' The village is Saint Jean de la Porte, in the foothills of the French Alps.
At its centre stands this property, opposite the Mairie and the local bar-restaurant.
On a clear day, the Mont Blanc is visible in the distance. Jean himself lives in the
neighbouring village of Saint Pierre d'Albigny where he runs the grapevine nursery
founded by his grandfather in the 1920s. He and his son Philippe also operate
the family vineyard in Saint Pierre (some 11 hectares of local varietals). His aim
when he bought this house was to go it alone: leave the local wine cooperative
and bottle wines under his own label. In 2000 he did just that, rewarding
a concerted family effort that ate up every weekend and holiday for five
years. Jean, his wife Christiane and two children, then still at school, turned
a dilapidated, leaky property with derelict outhouses and ragged vines into
what is now Domaine de Méjane.

The vineyard today is confined to a two-hectare *clos* alongside the house, most of
the original holding having been sold off piecemeal by the estate's former owners. The farm
is also long gone. But otherwise the property has been restored to its 18th-century founding
purpose – winegrowing – complete with a brand new winemaking facility, tasting cellar
and reception area. Equally important, it serves as a test bed and conservatory for ancient
Savoyard varietals in danger of extinction – such as the Persan, a Méjane speciality.

Since 2003 the estate has been run by Jean's daughter Anne and her husband Michael.
'This was always Anne's ambition,' says Jean – whose own ambition as a winegrower and
father was to pass on his passion to his children, for their sake and for the sake of the region
that bred them. 'The Domaine now feeds eight people,' he says proudly, 'our family plus
three salaried staff.' This is quite an achievement in a region now better known for ski
resorts than vineyards, where often deserted dormitory villages are now sadly on the
increase. *Phylloxera Vastatrix* is partly to blame. By the 1900s the region's vineyards had
dwindled to just 2,000 hectares, which is how they stand today. 'But it's also the mentality
that has changed – the lure of the town, the belief that life somehow owes you a living...'
Jean's own children have compelling reasons to stay put.

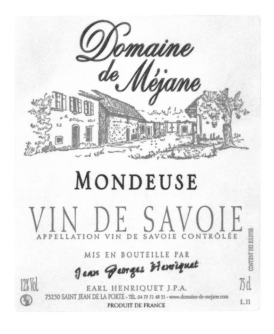

Above: Label from Méjane's
'Mondeuse' red wine, which is also
available in an oak-aged version.
The label is an engraving based
on Jean's design, showing the inner
courtyard with – from left to right –
the house, the *cuverie*, the bread oven
(fully functioning and still used by
Christiane) and the administration/
reception buildings.

Opposite: The kitchen-cum-
dining-room, an immense 3,500
sq ft (320 sq m), space that faces
north like the house itself. This
represents roughly a tenth of the
total living area and is the only
living space so far refurbished
(along with the bathroom, office
and main bedroom). Still to do are
the 5,700 sq ft (530 sq m) sitting
room and four more bedrooms.
In the vase is a spray of gingko
leaves and berries from an ancient
gingko, which grows in front of
the house along with a cedar and
200-year-old yew tree.

Opposite, above:
A classical example of a Dauphinoise – the house is stone-built with white shutters and a grey slate roof, all renovated in line with strict conservation rules. Towering behind is the 3,800 ft (1,150 m) Montlambert, at the heart of the Massif des Bauges Regional Park.

Opposite, below, left:
These outbuildings belong to Jean's neighbour, but the view of woodlands and thickets is a pleasure for all to share.

Opposite, below, right:
The cat 'Roussette', a present from Anne's in-laws. The name means 'ginger', but also pays tribute to the varietal used in the estate's Roussette de Savoie white wine.

Right: The main corridor, with flagstone floor, ribbed vaulted ceiling and whitewashed walls. The wood in the barrow is for the house's wood-burning stove. The corridor runs north–south for the entire length of the house, opening into the sitting room.

Left and opposite, above: The sitting room, so far unfinished but wonderfully spacious and light. All of the furniture pictured here came with the house, including the mirror and chair (left). The elaborately carved sideboard and table (opposite, above) laden with wines are walnut, as is the door and the floor too (a combination of dark walnut and lighter pine). Walnut is very much the local wood, Grenoble being just 30 miles away. The immense fire surround is blue marble.

Opposite, near right: Three Méjane wines on show in the tasting room: Persan, Mondeuse and Jacquère. The Méjane range is produced under three different AOCs (Vins de Savoie, Saint Jean de la Porte and Roussette de Savoie) and reflects the unusual variety of Savoie's appellations and sub-appellations. Bottlings include five red wines, three whites, one rosé and two sparkling whites.

Opposite, far right: Close-up of carving on sideboard, depicting a boar-hunting scene. Jean himself does not hunt, and his golden Labrador Sammy has no opinion on the matter.

THE RHÔNE VALLEY

JEAN-LOUIS CHAVE

There is no grand house here. The greatness of this estate rests entirely with its vineyards, and a winegrowing tradition that has passed down through 16 successive generations of the Chave family. It all started with a small parcel of land in the Ardèche, gifted to the original Jean-Louis Chave in 1481. From these small beginnings grew a family wine business that ranks today as one of the oldest – and perhaps greatest – father-to-son holdings in France. The 15th-century farmhouse where their ancestors lived for 300 years is now the Chave's country retreat. Constructed in the traditional Ardèchois style, the house is emblematic of a family that has always shunned the limelight. Now based in Mauves, some 12 miles further south, the Chave winery has no open-door policy. Gérard Chave – the only head of house not christened 'Jean-Louis' since 1481 – lives just next door, in the modest village house that has been the family home since the early 19th century. Guests and VIPs are accommodated in a newly renovated village house with the accent on simplicity and comfort.

The real showcase for this estate lies a few miles to the north, across a rickety footbridge over the Rhône, on the granite hill of Hermitage. On terrain as steep as this, the thin layer of topsoil must be contained within terraces to prevent erosion. Most of the ploughing is still done by horses, and the rest is down to human toil. 'For a winegrower, few *terroirs* are as genuinely humbling as this one,' says the present J-L Chave, Gérard's son. He employs one labourer per hectare on the hill – that's six times the manpower required in conventionally farmed vineyards on flat terrain. He and his young family live right at the top of the slope, in the *climat* (vineyard) known as l'Hermite. 'Last winter was the first time I really understood the meaning of "snowed in",' recalls Erin, his American-born wife from Missouri. The house is still not fully renovated – 'a bit like camping on a building site,' says Erin – but the views in every direction are sensational: to the east, the forest-capped hills of the Vercors; to the west, the Chapelle de l'Hermitage; and to the south, the River Rhône. And right there, on the doorstep so to speak, are the vineyards that are the Chave's pride and joy.

Jean-Louis officially joined the business in 1992, having finally realized that this was where his passion and duty lay. The winemaking philosophy remains unchanged – to make wines that do justice to their fabulous *terroir*, with the emphasis firmly on continuity, 'I haven't "taken over" from my father. I have simply picked up where he left off. It is the same journey for both of us.' Gérard is still very much the *éminence grise*. What matters in the end is not the man but the wine and the *terroir* it expresses. 'There is no room for ego in the service of wine,' says Jean-Louis. 'It isn't Chave we make here – it's Hermitage.'

The hill of Hermitage rises above the town of Tain, on the right bank of the Rhône. It is said to be named after the crusader-turned-hermit who built a chapel of retreat here in the early 13th century, also growing the very first grapes. Some of these vines are aged 100 years or more. For instance the Chave's Marsanne plot in the Péleat *climat*, which was bought by Gérard Chave in the 1930s and has not been replanted since. Chave Hermitage plantings consist of roughly nine hectares of Syrah (average age 40 years) and five of white vines (80 per cent Marsanne and 20 per cent Roussanne, with an average age of 50 years).

Left: The kitchen of the house in Mauves where the Chaves entertain their guests. 'This is a kitchen for people who like to cook – my father, for instance,' says Jean-Louis. Well-equipped, with good lighting, the room has a functional simplicity that we also see in the dining-room (below). The oak table can seat 30 guests and was constructed by an old friend of the family.

Opposite: A glass of Hermitage 2006. And the taste? 'White pepper, spice, red-berry fruit.' One senses that Jean-Louis is a doer, not a talker, and a firm believer that wines should be swallowed and not spat out.

Above: In the farmhouse in the Ardèche, home of the original Jean-Louis Chave, the kitchen is as plain as you would expect of a vigneron's house – dark oak furniture, white-washed walls.

Left: An oak bed in the master bedroom, slept in by 'Monsieur et Madame Chave' for three centuries.

Opposite: Inner courtyard of the farmhouse, hung with Virginia creeper and shaded by an ancient Acacia tree. Beyond the gateway, in the hills around Lemps, lies the original family vineyard. Known locally as 'Bachasson', it extends today over five hectares.

DOMAINE DE L'ORATOIRE SAINT MARTIN

The coat of arms of the village of Cairanne displays the motto 'Semper Augusta', which loosely translated means 'always in pursuit of greatness'. Looking out from the top of the ancient ramparts, the source of that inspiration is there for all to see. Row upon row of vines march across the landscape, surrounded by a majestic panorama of mountains. To the east are the Dentelles de Montmirail, foothills of the mighty Mont Ventoux that rises naked above them. To the west are the Cévennes. To the south are the glittering Alpilles with the Baux de Provence at their heart. It is this heroic landscape that brothers Frédéric and François Alary seek to express in their wines – a mission that has defined the destiny of the Alary family for more than 300 years.

The vineyards first planted by their forebear André Alary in the late 17th century now encompass some 28 hectares of organic plantings, located in the hills of Saint Martin, less than a mile from the family home in Cairanne. As present occupant Frédéric Alary points out, all of his predecessors once lived in the house he lives in today: there have been Alarys at this address since 1692. His sole experience of life away from Cairanne was as a military conscript in Nice. A quarter of a century later, he still retains memories of the city's culinary delights – as one might expect of a man whose livelihood depends on his sense of smell and taste. 'Frédéric has the most amazing olfactory memory,' says Monique, his wife of 25 years. 'It's fascinating to watch him taste wine, peeling away each layer of flavour, putting a name to every aroma by matching it to one of the hundreds of references stored in his brain.' Frédéric is a man of few words, with the single-minded dedication of someone in his chosen profession – winemaking. His other love is chess.

Winemaking on these premises spans three centuries and ten generations of Alary menfolk, 'but we couldn't have done it without the women,' says Frédéric. His grandmother, the lyrically named Venise Séraphine, was a case in point. It was her husband, also called Frédéric, who built the stone oratory for which the estate was named in the 1950s. It sits in the middle of the vineyard, a shrine to the herculean achievements of people like … his wife, for instance. A peasant woman born and bred, she proved better built for this kind of life than her husband, a man whose fragile constitution inclined him more towards intellectual pursuits. So she handled the plough, and he handled sales.

Frédéric and François joined the business in 1984, working alongside their father Bernard until his death in 1991. Frédéric, the elder brother by just 11 months, is now in charge of winemaking, while François operates the vineyards. 'Our aim is to express the *terroir* as it really is, with no holds barred,' says Frédéric. 'But we have only one lifetime, and a lifetime is too short.' This is not to deny the rewards they have earned for such devoted effort. The wines they produce today are ranked among the finest of all the Côte du Rhône offerings.

Above: Wine label of the 'Cuvée Prestige' Cairanne. The wine is a 60/40 blend of organically grown Grenache and Mourvèdre grapes, from ancient vines first planted in 1905 and not replanted since. The Grenache and Mourvèdre are still planted together in the traditional manner, but never mixed with other varieties.

Opposite, above: The family home in Cairanne, at the foot of the old village. On the ground floor around the courtyard are the aging cellars, tasting room/reception facilities and offices.

Opposite, below: A barrowful of flowers (left)… Monique's birthday present from her husband. The wheelbarrow was handmade by a craftsman in the Alps. View south (right), looking towards the old village of Cairanne and the former donjon of the Knights Hospitallers (top right).

Above: The dining room, featuring an oak *pannetière* (baking table) complete with a drawer to store the yeast. Above, also in oak, is a traditional bread cabinet. The picture on the wall (top left) is by a local artist, showing Cairanne's 13th-century Chapelle Notre Dame des Excès, built at the time of the great plague. The fortified village itself dates back to the Knights Hospitallers (12th century) and retains much of its original medieval architecture.

Top: Pewter wine-bottle holder, on the dresser in the family dining room. The wine is a Cairanne rouge 'Haut-Coustias'.

Above: Four generations of Alary winegrowers. Clockwise from the left: local historian Frédéric Alary, grandfather of Frédéric and François, architect of the oratory; Michel Alary, the boys' great-grandfather; Denis Alary, the boys' great-great-grandfather; and finally the boys' father, Bernard Alary.

CHÂTEAU FORTIA

If France had not passed the law of 1905 separating Church and State then the outlook for French wine might have been quite different. Baron Pierre Le Roy de Boiseaumarie (1890–1967) would have served his country like all of his forebears, following in the footsteps of his crusading ancestors. Instead he took up law. France's secularization alienated a good many Catholics, the Baron's father among them, who vowed that neither they nor their descendants would ever again serve the State. In the event, his son Pierre did become a national hero, decorated for his bravery as a fighter pilot in the First World War. On his return he married Château Fortia heiress, Edmée Bernard Le Saint, and in 1923, legal skills to the fore, he spearheaded a voluntary appellation system aimed at regulating the quality of Châteauneuf wines. This became the framework for the AOC laws of the early 1930s that have largely defined French (and indeed world) wine production ever since.

Châteauneuf-du-Pape is the flagship of the southern Rhône appellation, already renowned for its wines when the papacy moved to Avignon in around 1316. The popes indeed were particular fans of the local wine, but as Château Fortia managing director Pierre Pastre dryly points out, 'local wine was all there was in those days'. His wife Chantal is the granddaughter of Baron Le Roy. With a background in agrichemicals, Pierre himself is engagingly matter of fact about the business of wine – except for the debt owed to his wife's grandfather.

Châteauneuf-du-Pape was one of the first areas to receive AOC designation (on 21 November 1933) and is said to boast some of the strictest standards in the world. 'A far cry from the sorry situation that awaited the Baron when he settled here in 1919,' observes Pierre Pastre. Centuries of fraud, compounded by *Phylloxera Vastatrix* and four years of neglect in the First World War had left a region in crisis. The Baron championed its recovery, also co-founding the OIV (Office International du Vin) and the INAO (Institut National des Appellations d'Origine) – an initiative that wisely anticipated today's global wine market.

Chantal and her brothers, Thierry and Bruno Le Roy (solidly supported by their aunt 'Tante Vivette'), are the fourth generation to run this estate since it was acquired in 1890 by their maternal great-grandfather Bernard Le Saint. The house's neo-Gothic style dates from then but the oldest parts are 14th century. The vineyard too is ancient, extending in a single block around the property, some 31 hectares in all, in a *terroir* famous for its *galets roulés*: large quartz pebbles from ancient riverbeds where mammoths once frolicked. Several parcels here were first planted in the 17th century, making this one of the oldest estates in Châteauneuf.

Opposite: The style of the house is typical French Gothic Revival (as famously championed by French architect Viollet-le-Duc): slate roof, bullseye windows, octagonal tower. 'A style adopted by town halls all over Paris,' says Pierre Pastre. Pictured in the foreground is a *Sophora Japonica* dating from the house's acquisition by Bernard Le Saint in 1890. Visible bottom right are geraniums and oleanders that embellish the smaller of two interconnecting terraces (see overleaf).

Below: Wine label designed by Bernard Le Saint and still used today for certain wines. The main change to the house since then is the roof extension (on the right of the tower) added by Pierre's in-laws when they moved here in the late 1960s.

Château Fortia Réserve 2007

Châteauneuf-du-Pape

APPELLATION CHÂTEAUNEUF-DU-PAPE CONTRÔLÉE

15% alc./vol.   *Mis en bouteille au Château*   750 ml

Château Fortia sarl, Propriétaire Récoltant à Châteauneuf-du-Pape - 84230 France

Propriété du Baron Le Roy

PRODUCT OF FRANCE   PRODUIT DE FRANCE

Left: The 'grande terrasse', reached from the 'petite terrasse' (see preceding pages). South-facing and sheltered from the Mistral, it provides ideal conditions for oleanders and hollyhocks, which thrive in the dappled shade of an ancient Plane Tree Maple (planted by Bernard Le Saint).

Opposite: The 'grand hall': a passageway leading to bedrooms that also serves as a reception area when the house is full of people – a reminder that Château Fortia was traditionally just a summer residence. The bookcases are pure French Pompadour style (18th century), added by Baron Le Roy's daughter, Viviane (twin sister of 'Tante Vivette') shortly before her death in 1976. The tables, chairs and mosaic flooring are typically Provençal – time-worn furnishings with the patina of generations past.

Above: The chiaroscuro *caveau de dégustation* (tasting cellar) dates from the 14th century when the house was first built. The furnishings are slightly younger: 17th-century Louis XIII high-back armchair, and 16th-century Henri II walnut sideboard (left). The ghostly presence surveying the proceedings is a lost-wax mould used to cast a bust of Baron Le Roy for the village of Sainte Cécile les Vignes, roughly about 25 miles away.

Right: Vaulted passageway to the cask chamber, one of three interconnecting chambers that make up the château cellars. All Château Fortia wines see wood, with the reds accounting for the lion's share of plantings: 27 hectares compared to just three hectares of white varietals. The red wines are driven by the Grenache Rouge (70%) and the whites by the Clairette (60%).

Left: Baron Pierre Le Roy de Boiseaumarie – who agreed to represent local producers (in 1923), but only on condition that they themselves set an example by their honesty and discipline. Pictured here is the medal struck in his honour in 1975 by the Châteauneuf-du-Pape winegrowers syndicate.

PROVENCE

CHÂTEAU DE SAINT MARTIN

In 1929 the first ever women-only car rally rolled out of Paris, headed for a finish on the other side of France. When the chequered flag fell in Saint Raphael our intrepid lady drivers had covered more than 800 miles. The race, called the 'Paris–St Raphael Féminin', was the brainchild of famous wine personality, Count Edmé de Rohan-Chabot, father of the Comtesse de Gasquet who owns this estate today. Into a long succession of women, comes a man who was himself one of their greatest admirers. Otherwise, the château has passed from mother to daughter since its foundation in 1740.

At the helm today is Adeline de Barry, the Countess' daughter. 'This house is full of stories,' she says. 'The Count, my grandfather, loved pretty women as much as he loved fast cars – a "women-only" car rally meant he could feast his eyes on both!' Another ancestor left a very amusing written record of turbulent pre-revolutionary France – before dying in 1792 defending the young King Louis XVI at the Tuileries Palace. His 14-year-old son then walked all the way back here from Paris to rejoin his mother. Adeline, with four children of her own, has a strong sense of family duty. 'My role is to maintain a chain that extends back hundreds of years, acknowledging that what I am today is largely owed to being part of something much bigger than myself. My children feel rooted in Saint Martin. But if they do one day decide to take up the baton, it won't be for money, that's for sure. You don't get rich running an estate like this.' In 1997 severe frost wiped out 80 per cent of her grape crop overnight. 'It took us more than three years to get back on our feet.'

Perhaps this is a small price to pay for the timelessness that pervades this estate, in an area that has attracted settlement since prehistoric times. The avenue leading up to the property is a branch road of the Via Aurelia, originally connecting Rome with Arles. In the château precincts are the vestiges of a Gallo-Roman villa occupied from the 2nd century BC to the 7th century AD. Our story begins here: in vineyards first planted by the Romans, then lovingly tended for 800 years by the monks of Lérins. Their impressive subterranean cellars, dug into rock, survive to this day. In 1740 the estate was sold to a private buyer whose daughter and new husband (Adeline's ancestor) picked up where the monks left off. 'The château dates from then, built as a gift for the lucky bride – a far cry from the leaky property I took over in 1986,' recalls Adeline. Now restored to 18th-century glory, the château consists of a central section with wings to either side. The atmosphere is distinctly Provence, with centuries-old plane trees dappling a red ochre façade and blue louvered shutters closed tight against the blind blue sky. The wines, too, voice their Mediterranean origins loud and clear.

Opposite: The southern façade, looking out over English-style landscape gardens first planted by Adeline's ancestor in 1740. The house is shaded by Plane trees and *Micocouliers*, a tree typical of the region and variously known as the Lotus Tree, Mediterranean Nettle Tree and Hackberry, among others.

Left: From one countess to another … the 'Comtesse de Saint Martin' old-vines bottling, created by Adeline in honour of all her lady predecessors. One of just 23 Crus Classés in the Côtes de Provence AOC (out of more than 1,000 producers), Château de Saint Martin has never followed the crowd. 'This is Provence,' says Adeline, 'home of dazzling paintings, flowery literature and richly coloured wines. When pale rosé became all the rage, ours remained unashamedly pink.'

Right: Reception room to the left of the main entrance (which is glimpsed through the doors). The magnificent nautical-themed tapestry is 15th–16th century. Bathed in natural light all year round, the space is ablaze with colours that echo the vibrant tones of the tapestry – Mediterranean blue doors, red upholstery and a gamut of ochres and browns. The furnishings are of the period.

Left: The Chambre du Marquis, one of four *chambres d'hôte* on the first floor, with views to the east and south. Trees lend shade to the south-facing aspect, creating an intimate ambiance steeped in the patina of centuries past. Pictured in the foreground is a period *secrétaire à abattant* (drop-leaf desk), with canopied bed in the background. The château is scrupulously maintained, using only traditional finishes and furnishings.

Right: Bedside water presented in carafe with glasses in the Chambre du Marquis. 'So much more agreeable than a plastic bottle of mineral water,' says Adeline.

Below: The Chambre Juigné (a family name). This large and romantic room was used in 2007 as one of the settings for a French film based on *John Thomas and Lady Jane*, D. H. Lawrence's alternative version of *Lady Chatterley's Lover*, published nearly half a century later in 1972.

CHÂTEAU VANNIÈRES

Green lawns, pine trees and a distinctly Scottish-looking castle are not what one expects to find just 25 miles from Marseilles. And yet, for all its seeming incongruity, Château Vannières sits comfortably within its setting, at the heart of a region that has been producing wine for more than two millennia. The nearby village of Castellet overlooks steeply terraced vineyards that were first planted by the Phocaeans in the 6th century BC. From there, vine growing gradually spread throughout the Mediterranean Basin and then northwards and eastwards into the rest of France. The estate now owned by Eric Boisseaux and his mother dates back to the 16th century, founded by the Sieur de Lombard, Lord of Castellet. The Scottish-style castle we see here dates from the 18th century, designed by a Scotsman called … Scott. It is built on top of the original 16th-century property which now houses the cellars, winery and office space. Mr Scott also continued to make wine, furthering the reputation of vineyards that were among the first to win AOC classification in 1941.

The Bandol AOC has retained that distinction ever since, feted by critics as 'the Pauillac of Provence'. For the uninitiated, Pauillac is home to some of the finest Bordeaux wines – 'and when it comes to Bandol, they don't come much finer than Château Vannières', claims one British wine expert. For his American counterpart, the nose of a good Vannières actually bears an uncanny resemblance to a Pauillac. 'Or indeed, to a great Burgundy from the Côte de Nuits,' adds Eric Boisseaux, whose views may seem like heresy to die-hard fans of Bordeaux and Burgundy respectively. But then, he should know. Originally from Beaune, Eric was born into an old-established family of wine merchants with holdings in Beaujolais and the Rhône Valley. Château Vannières entered the family fold in 1957, purchased by Eric's grandfather, Lucien Boudot. His daughter, Eric's mother, then ran all three estates following her husband's untimely death in 1968. Thrown in at the deep end, Eric has been in the wine business ever since: 'officially since the age of 19, unofficially since I was 12.' His own son, who is an only child like his father, will take over when Eric retires. He too acquired his winemaking credentials in Beaune.

'We used to come here every summer when I was small,' muses Eric, recalling the family's seaside holidays in Bandol: the smell of the Mediterranean, the feel of the sand on bare feet unaccustomed to being shoeless… His mother still lives in the château, with Eric committed fulltime to Château Vannières since 1991. The vineyard runs to some 47 hectares, of which 33 hectares are in production, planted to Mourvèdre, Grenache and Cinsault (for red wines) and Clairette and Rolle (for white wines). The average age of the vines is 35 years and the planting methods are in accordance with 'viticulture raisonnée'. Pruning and vineyard management are in the best Bandol tradition, with the same vignerons returning every year to tend the same vines. Eric's oldest vignerons have been with him for 20 years.

The results speak for themselves. Eric Boisseaux combines a genuine passion for his work with the articulate enthusiasm of a seasoned professional. 'Great wines, born of a perfect marriage of grape and *terroir*, evolve in ways that defy the expectations of their makers,' he says. 'The main threat to their survival today is not globalization as one might imagine, but the outrageous mark-ups applied by the restaurant trade.'

Château Vannières derives its name from the women basket-weavers (*vannières*) who worked in this area in the 16th century, using the reeds that still grow in the streams around the property. Madame Boisseaux, Eric's mother, inherited the house from her father in 1968. Just three weeks later, her husband suffered a fatal car accident and she took over as winemaker. She never remarried, she says, and wine was thereafter 'her only passion'. Now it's her son's turn, she taking charge of events, tastings and receptions. 'I have more than enough to keep me busy!'

Above: South-facing
terrace, shaded by ancient
pine trees that include
a 500-year-old specimen
growing on the terrace
itself. The furnishings
are contemporary, chosen
by Mme Boisseaux and
perfectly in keeping
with their outdoor setting.
Much as she loves antiques,
she is 'all in favour of
a bit of modernization
now and then.'

Left: The main reception
room, featuring Louis XV
gilded wood carved console
and pair of Louis XVI
armchairs. The straighter,
more angular style is
characteristic of Louis XVI.

Right: A pretty Louis XV chest and two cabriolet armchairs, one occupied by the family's late Yorkshire terrier, in the main reception room. The room owes much of its grace and charm to Mme Boisseaux' ambitious refurbishments. Gone are the original *tomette* floor tiles (pictured overleaf in the entrance hall), replaced by a white marble floor with mother-of-pearl Cabochon inlays. The exposed ceiling beams are also now concealed, adding a lighter, more modern touch that flatters the gracious 18th-century furnishings.

Left: The main entrance, with 18th-century statue and Louis XVI furnishings. The *tomette* floor tiles are original (continuing up the staircase), but the entrance itself, rebuilt by Mme Boisseaux, was originally a much smaller affair.

Above, left: Château Vannières, Bandol AOC red, from vineyards planted to the traditional grape varieties: Mourvèdre and Grenache (for red wines); Grenache, Cinsault and Mourvèdre (for rosés); and Clairette and Bourboulenc (for white wines).

Above, right: The 16th-century cellars, constructed by the Lord of Castellet who originally founded this estate. The casks contain slowly maturing red wine, which is left to age here for two years before bottling.

Right: The steps that lead to the 'Boutique à vin', housed in the 16th-century building along with the winery, cellars, offices and – more recently – a brand new reception area that occupies a chamber uncovered when the ceiling fell through due to violent rains.

MAS DE LA DAME

Legend has it that this house, tucked at the foot of Les Baux in deepest Provence, was named after a fair maiden who lost her lover to the Crusades. In truth, the 'dame' of the Mas de la Dame was Hélène Hugolène, owner of this estate in the 15th century. Whether she and our bereft maiden were one and the same, we shall never know.

Six centuries later history would repeat itself, intruding on the destinies of present owners, sisters Caroline Missoffe and Anne Poniatowski. 'Our father's unexpected death in 1988, at the age of only 67, was a great shock to all of us,' remembers Caroline. 'Neither my sister nor I had any experience of this kind of life. We were both journalists, living and working in Paris, married with children. But letting go of the estate was unthinkable. The Mas de la Dame had been part of our lives since childhood, the place where we spent every holiday, first as children ourselves, then as mothers with children of our own.'

It took them just under ten years to make the change, reinventing themselves as talented professionals 'capable of making good wine'. Was it worth it? 'Definitely,' says Caroline. 'We love what we do; we love the place – and that's why we took it on. No regrets.' At the helm since 1995, the sisters are the fourth generation of this family to uphold the legacy of their grandfather Robert Faye, founder of the first estate in the Baux Valley to combine wine with olive-oil production. Total holdings now comprise some 300 hectares, planted to 57 hectares of vineyards and 28 of olive groves, extending in a single block along the southern flank of the Alpilles. Much of this area is land reclaimed from the *garrigue* by Robert Faye, extending the estate purchased by his father, Auguste, in 1903. 'Most of what you see today is our grandfather's handiwork,' explains Caroline, 'He bought up adjoining plots, clearing, planting and re-planting as necessary. He also restored the house, converting it from a "mas" in the most literal sense – with animal stalls at one end and family living quarters at the other – into a house fit for human habitation.'

In his 12-month stay as a voluntary mental patient in Saint Rémy de Provence, Vincent van Gogh painted the Mas de la Dame. The painting remains the emblem of this estate, reproduced from a photograph supplied by the painting's owner and now displayed on every wine label. The work itself has meanwhile disappeared, stolen exactly 100 years later while on loan for an exhibition. Faye's vision for this estate has plainly withstood the test of time, pursued with equal commitment today by his granddaughters. All their wines and olive oils are produced from organically grown fruit and sales continue to climb despite the recession. 'This is no time to be cutting corners,' insists Caroline. 'Now, more than ever, we aim to harness the full potential of this *terroir*, using organic farming methods that respect time-honoured traditions. Laborious maybe, but certainly rewarding.'

Above: Wine label of the Mas de la Dame Réserve du Mas red – a blend of Grenache, Syrah and Cabernet Sauvignon from a *terroir* deep in the heart of the *garrigue*.

Opposite: The medieval village of Les Baux de Provence, carved out of the rock of the Alpilles Mountains, more than 1,000 ft (300 m) above sea level. Rising above it (on the left of the picture) is the former stronghold of the Lords of Baux, an ideal place from which to pour boiling oil on unwelcome visitors. The village is named after the rocky spur on which it stands (*baou* in Provençal) and eventually gave its name to *bauxite* (aluminium ore) that was discovered here in 1821 by geologist Pierre Berthier. The old village, at its peak, was home to 4,000 souls, now reduced to just 22.

Above, left: The Mas de la Dame today is a sensitively renovated property, combining all the charm of its 16th-century origins with the comforts of 21st-century living. The house that so dazzled Vincent van Gogh has lost none of its appeal, set amid timeless hillsides of thyme and wild fennel.

Above, right: One of three boundary stones that were prudently restored by Robert Faye, bearing in mind a Nostradamus prediction that a great tidal wave would come crashing to a halt at one of these stones. This one is on the path leading up to the Mas; the second is at the entrance to the main courtyard, and the third is at the junction of the roads to Les Baux and Saint Rémy (which happens to be the birthplace of Nostradamus).

Above: Stone table in the small courtyard, with a selection of Mas de la Dame bottlings and home-grown fare – olives, figs and locally baked *pain de campagne*. The Lords of Baux could not have asked for more.

Right: Window of a now-renovated outbuilding in the main courtyard.

Opposite and above:
Bust of Robert Faye, overlooked by portrait of his father Auguste, in stone niche in the 'grande salle voûtée' (main living space with vaulted ceiling). The former stables, kitchen and mill room are now a 260-metre square living space, made spacious by white walls, vaulted ceiling, uncluttered furnishings and natural materials. Still in place is the original olive press (too heavy to move elsewhere), which with the years has come to resemble some huge, abstract modern sculpture. 'We all love this room, with its vaulted ceilings and massive fireplace,' enthuses Caroline. 'It brings back happy memories of childhood Christmases, gathered round the fire with all our cousins and aunts and uncles … Christmas in Provence is still a very special time for me.'

CORSICA

CLOS CAPITORO

'Capitoro' is Corsican for 'bull's head'. They say this estate is named after a local chieftain who wore a horned helmet as a symbol of his power and bull-like ferocity. The Corsicans, of course, are famous for their indomitable spirit, especially when it comes to matters of sovereignty. Actually, their only experience of independence was the short-lived Corsican Republic (1755–69) – little more than a hiccup in an otherwise uninterrupted history of occupation that started with the Ancient Greeks and continues today with the French. But nationalist feeling still runs high, proving that independence is like Corsica itself: once experienced, never forgotten. No one knows this better than Clos Capitoro owner, Jacques Bianchetti, who is mayor of the commune of Cauro and uniquely placed to champion his country's interests. He learned from the best. His grandfather, also called Jacques, earned his place in Corsican history as the saviour of local viticulture following the ravages of *Phylloxera Vastatrix*. Inadvertently introduced to Europe in 1865 via imported North American vines, *Phylloxera Vastatrix* was ultimately overcome by the use of disease-resistant American rootstock. But the immediate French reaction was to ban all imported vines, particularly those from North America.

Trained agronomist Jacques Bianchetti found a way round the problem by growing his own disease-resistant rootstock from seeds – for his own benefit and that of the entire Corsican winegrowing community. In 1907 he was decorated by France for his 'meritorious services to agriculture'. The family vineyards he saved from extinction now extend across 50 hectares, fanned by cooling mountain breezes and milder air from the Mediterranean. A few miles to the south is Ajaccio, birthplace of Napoleon Bonaparte; a few miles to the north is Calvi, which, according to legend, was the birthplace of Christopher Columbus. So the man who reinvented France and the man who discovered the Americas were born within just a short distance of each other. At roughly the same time as Columbus set sail in 1492, the first Bianchettis arrived in Corsica from Italy – and here they have remained ever since. The estate now operated by Jacques Bianchetti has been producing wine since the early 1800s, known then and now as the Clos

Capitoro. The owner at the time was a certain Martin Bianchetti, a Catholic priest who bequeathed the holding to his nephew Louis Bianchetti. In 1856 the Clos Capitoro bottled the first wine under its own label, which was designed by Louis and is still the label today. The house itself dates from around 1800, as pungently Corsican in style as the island's emblematic grape, the Sciaccarellu. 'A good taster,' says Jacques Bianchetti, 'can always tell an Ajaccio wine from that unmistakable bouquet of red berries, plums and smouldering maquis that are the signature of the Sciaccarellu – a varietal found nowhere else in the world.'

Opposite: The southern façade, overlooking the glittering waters of the Bay of Ajaccio. The view to the north looks out over a Tuscan-like landscape of vineyards, bordered by the Massif du Renoso with more mountains beyond. Pictured in the foreground are two centenarian olive trees, the one on the right entwined with Jasmine that thrives in Corsica's virtually frost-free climate. The lush green lawn is a real tour de force in this mountainous, Mediterranean environment.

Above: Jacques Bianchetti has modernized the property considerably since he took over some 30 years ago. Pictured here is the east-facing conservatory, built by Jacques for his elderly mother who lives with him. On the table in the foreground is a bottle of the multi-award winning Clos Capitoro Rosé.

Right: Clos Capitoro Rouge, based on the Sciaccarellu, perfect with Corsican sheep's cheese.

Opposite: Roughly 40,000 bottles are laid down in the *chai* (wine storehouse) for at least two years. The estate is currently experimenting with wood aging, but Jacques remains unconvinced. 'The Sciaccarellu has plenty of aromas of its own,' he says.

Above: The clay statuettes are Jacques' handiwork, displayed here in the living room on the ground floor.

Right: An early 20th-century guide to the making of fortified wines, first used by the original Jacques Bianchetti, and still used today by his namesake.

LANGUEDOC-ROUSSILLON

CHÂTEAU DE JAU

'It is the custom in France,' explains owner Sabine Dauré, 'to call an old-established wine estate like ours a "château", but to me this house is not a château, it is my home. When I think of this house, I think of my friends, of summer evenings on the terrace, of the year we staged an opera on the tennis court, and of the many artists who have exhibited their works here.' When Sabine's husband, Bernard, and his brother acquired the estate in 1974 from a Roussillon wine merchant they brought with them six generations of Catalan winemaking tradition. Sabine brought her love of the arts – a passion that was to establish Jau as one of the first, if not *the* first ever, wineries to accommodate a contemporary art gallery within its precincts.

The Roussillon, back then, was famous for many things – Romanesque architecture, Cathar castles and *vins doux naturels* in particular – but modern art was not one of them. This region is no stranger to change, however, having lived through successive occupations before it was finally annexed to France in the 17th century.

The Agly Valley, where the house stands, borders the Aude department, in the heart of Catalan country. The valley winds its way through centuries-old vineyards and olive groves, along the former frontier between Aragon and France. Château de Jau nestles in the foothills of the Corbières Mountains, built on the site of a 12th-century Cistercian abbey. Its defiantly 'maison de maître' style seems to thumb its nose at the Republican ideals that marked the years of its construction: 1789. Some 40 miles away are the yoke-shaped hills after which the abbey was named: 'Jau' is a contraction of *jugum*, the Latin term for yoke.

The Jau contemporary art space housed in the former *magnanerie* (silk-worm nursery) opened its doors in 1977. The restaurant was established soon afterwards, prompted by a visit from France's then First Lady, Anne-Aymone Giscard d'Estaing. 'I was asked to provide lunch when she came to see Tautavel Man,' recalls Sabine, 'but I couldn't think what to feed her. It was our friend and *cuisine nouvelle* guru Michel Guérard who suggested rustic vigneron fare – *pan boli* (bread rubbed with garlic, olive oil and tomato), lamb cutlets and sausages grilled over grapevine cuttings. After that, every other visitor who came to the gallery expected to be fed – and what nicer way to spend the day than in an idyllic setting, feasting the eyes and nourishing the body!'

The Gril de Jau restaurant stands in the shade of a 300-year-old mulberry tree. It is run today by Sabine's eldest daughter, Estelle, who is also in charge of the vineyards with her brother Simon. The menu still specializes in local vigneron fare.

The Jau vineyards have been entirely replanted and the estate has more than doubled in size. Many of the plateau and mid-hill parcels occupy land reclaimed from the *garrigue* in 1983. Bernard Dauré recalls with amusement how disbelieving locals would come every Sunday to gawp at 'the graveyard' – Grenache Noir and Carignan plantings that they thought did not stand a prayer. Thirty years on, those same plantings form part of a thriving patchwork of *terroirs*, swept by the Tramontane and salty sea breezes, all dedicated to traditional southern grape varieties. The wines they produce echo the link between art and vines that made this estate a pioneer in its time: the label for the estate's best-selling Jaja de Jau was specially designed by Italian-born French installation artist, Ben Vautier, more usually known as 'Ben'.

The house faces south, looking
out from the immense terrace
across vineyards and *garrigue*
all the way to the Corbières
Mountains. A boldly neo-
classical style combined with
warm ochres and reds gives
the château a decidedly Tuscan
look, helped by the chirruping
of cicadas in sentinel-like
Cypress trees.

Left: The entrance hall, with original staircase and marble floor. The entire ground floor is open plan – contemporary living in an 18th-century setting. On display are works of art by exhibitors at Jau, such as French artist Richard Fauguet who made this chandelier from recycled decanters and glasses.

Opposite, above, left: Archway, to inner courtyard, leading to the *mas* via an archway and courtyard beyond.

Opposite, above, right: The dining area, with painting by French abstract artist, Nîmes-born Claude Viallat – red squares on the wall, marble squares on the floor.

Opposite, below, left: Portrait of Monsieur Dauré senior in the library area, set against a book collection that is every bibliophile's dream. Rare books and first editions include Machiavelli's *The Prince* and Charles Jouet's *Le Tombeau de Charles Baudelaire*.

Opposite, below, right: Sculpture by Richard Venet, displayed here in the first of the inner courtyards pictured above.

Above: The living area, looking through to the dining area. The château had already been renovated several times when the Daurés moved here in the 1970s. They added their own style, 'looking to bring out that quintessential charm of old properties through a mixture of big, bold artworks and Old World influences.'

Opposite: Vibrant modern art and classic French furnishings meld with oriental fabrics and paper sculpture. Creativity works its magic, helped by high ceilings and tall windows that capture the luminosity of the southern light.

Left: First-floor landing, featuring an 'airmail painting' by Chilean artist Eugenio Dittborn – one of a series of large collages that 'collect meaning' as they travel around the world. The aim, says Dittborn, is to create visual 'Chinese whispers' – messages passed on and transformed in the process. The Daurés got to know Dittborn when staying at their Las Niñas winery in Chile's Apalta valley.

Above: South-facing terrace, attached to the eastern end of the house. It creates a transition from interior living spaces to the exterior world of mountains and *garrigue* – a shady haven from the sizzling heat of summer, looking out over the lunar landscapes of the Corbières that so inspired the Cathars in the 12th century.

Right: Wine label of the Jaja de Jau, designed by Italian-born French artist 'Ben' Vautier. Famous for his text-based paintings (rather like Dittborn), Ben is best known for his collage work entitled 'L'art est inutile. Rentrez chez vous.' (Art is useless. Go home.)

CHÂTEAU DE PENNAUTIER

Molière, the French playwright, once performed here for his patron Pierre-Louis de Pennautier, the son of Bernard de Pennautier who originally built the château in 1620. Tucked away in the archives is a receipt for the fee paid to Molière and his troop on that occasion – probably a fraction of the price fetched today for one of the château's stellar Cabardès wines.

Château de Pennautier, classified a 'monument historique', sits at a height of 720 ft (220 m) above sea level, commanding sweeping views of the Pyrenees to the south and the Massif Central to the north. Known as the 'Versailles of Languedoc', the property was enlarged in 1670 by royal architect Louis Le Vau. Complementing Le Vau's grandiose architecture are 30 hectares of formal gardens by French landscape designer André Le Nôtre (renowned for his work at Versailles, Chantilly, Fontainebleau and the Tuileries in Paris, to name but a few).

The Pennautiers were pioneering landowners, who contributed greatly to the development of the Languedoc. By the early 17th century, Pennautier wines shipped via the new Canal du Midi were popular at the court of the Sun King, Louis XIV. With glorious credentials such as these, the running of this enterprise is not for the fainthearted – as present owners Nicolas and Miren de Lorgeril knew when they took over in 1987. 'The challenge was to consolidate the hard work and achievements of our predecessors but also to move with the times,' says Miren. Determined to regain control of the estate's destinies, they no longer sell through *négociants* (wine merchants), but now handle all sales themselves. Total Lorgeril holdings encompass around 350 hectares under vine, planted in six family estates distributed across nine Languedoc AOCs. Most of the vineyards sprawl across the sunny flanks of the Montagne Noire, often on land reclaimed from the *garrigue* at altitudes approaching 1,200 ft (365 m).

The first ten years were make or break, says Miren. But by 1997 they knew they were home and dry – a real achievement for a couple with no previous experience of winery management. Nicolas is the tenth generation of his family to run this estate, but his background is in management, and Miren's is in law. 'Wine today is consumed throughout the world – that wasn't true in our parents' day. And it wouldn't have happened at all if people hadn't created new markets for wines by planting vineyards all over the world. The greater and more global the demand, the bigger the potential market for our own wines.'

The château today offers conference and other meeting and reception facilities. The interior decoration is as sumptuous as you would expect of a property of this standing: a wealth of furniture and design, recently renovated as part of a three-year programme of improvements that commenced in mid-2006. 'Our aim was to retain all of the building's original 18th-century charm and character,' explains Miren, 'but at no expense to 21st-century comfort!'

Left: Wine label from the Château de Pennautier Terroir d'Altitude bottling. The vines cling to steep, rocky slopes on the southern reaches of the Montagne Noire, at altitudes of 600–1,200 ft (180–365 m).

Above: Château de Pennautier's façade is characteristic of the Italian Baroque style that spread to France in the early 17th century. The east and west wings were added by royal architect Louis Le Vau in 1670, inspired by his colossal remodelling of the hunting lodge outside Paris that became the Palace of Versailles. The style is typical of Le Vau's more classical designs, for which the château was nicknamed 'Petit Versailles du Languedoc'. The triangular pediment on the centre of the façade is engraved with the Lorgeril coat of arms. The château faces south, overlooking Chardonnay plantings.

Opposite: The main entrance to the château, featuring a ceremonial staircase and mosaic floor dating from 1830. Here we see the refined classicism that distinguishes the French Baroque from its more exuberant Italian counterpart: sober sculptural values stripped of ostentatious decoration, and a subtle use of colour, light and shade.

Right: The Salon de Choiseul with Louis XV *bergère* and occasional table in the foreground. The walls were recently relined with Nobilis damask, as part of major renovations between 2006 and 2009.

Left: The Salon de Choiseul was named after the Duc de Choiseul (1719–85) whose portrait hangs on the wall. Etienne-François de Choiseul was a French military officer, diplomat and statesman during the reign of Louis XV. His fortunes owed much to the patronage of the King's mistress, Jeanne-Antoinette Poisson, Marquise de Pompadour, and declined with her untimely death from tuberculosis aged just 42. Beneath his portrait is a small *table de milieu* (mid-table) of Italian signature.

Above: The Salon de Madame, featuring Louis XV armchair and 18th-century bookcases lined with 18th- and 19th-century editions. Formerly the Salon Vert, the room is now named in honour of present owner Madame de Lorgeril. 'The salon is my favourite room in the château. It represents everything I love about great houses: history, glory and grandeur, but also that sense of intimacy that speaks to the emotions.'

Right: Close-up of 19th-century door fastener in the 'grand salon' on the first floor.

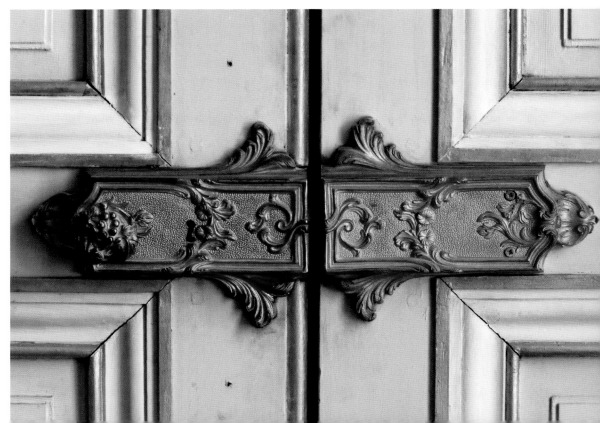

Above: The Chambre du Roi – bedchamber where Louis XIII slept on 14 July 1622. Classified a Monument Historique, the bed and matching furnishings formed part of his majesty's travel accoutrements.

Opposite: The Salon d'Honneur: in the foreground sits a tray laden with glasses of Château de Pennautier Terroir d'Altitude Rosé; in the background a Boule chest of drawers by André-Charles Boulle (or Boule), appointed royal Versailles cabinetmaker by Louis XIV.

Opposite: The Salon d'Honneur was where receptions and parties were traditionally concluded. The walls are covered with Lelièvre damask. In the foreground stands an Erard grand piano, while on the mantelpiece a bust of Queen Marie Antoinette casts an approving eye over the elegant surroundings.

Above and right: The Chambre Marmier, named like all of the bedrooms after a branch of the family tree, with a blue marble fireplace and Charles X furnishings. English hand-painted wallpaper features different views of Rome, such as the Piazza San Pietro (pictured in close-up, right). The doors connect with an en-suite bathroom.

ABBAYE DE VALMAGNE

Gothic columns soar heavenwards, merging in a celestial canopy of stone vaulting. Lodged in the arcade at their feet are 18 huge oak vats that serve as stolid reminders of earthly values. These vats were the saving of the magnificent Gothic church of Valmagne Abbey, constructed by the Cistercians in 1257 on the site of an early Romanesque chapel. The abbey itself is much older, founded in 1139 by Raymond Trencavel, Viscount of Béziers. The vats, installed in 1820, marked the end of the abbey's monastic vocation and the commencement of a secular calling that continues to this day. The wines they hold come from vineyards planted by the Cistercians in the 12th century and were produced by the abbey until the late 18th century – when the French Revolution intervened. Some 50 years later, with the vats in place and the lands under private ownership, the abbey was still standing – a lucky escape in a period that saw most of the monasteries in France stripped of their stone.

Present owner Diane de Gaudart d'Allaines recalls how the estate purchased in 1838 by her ancestor, the Count de Turenne, came with its own blacksmith, carpenter and builder. 'A complete team of craftsmen lived in tied cottages right here on the premises,' she explains. 'The accommodation was rudimentary to say the least: one-up-one-down, with shared amenities. As a child, I remember visiting the carpenter with my grandmother.' It's an entirely different situation today as they rely entirely on outside contractors and the smallest job seems to require permission from the Architectes des Monuments Historiques. 'People must think we are made of money… In the 21st century how many families can afford to take on a place like this?'

Valmagne Abbey is located some ten miles inland from Sète (France's largest Mediterranean fishing port), overlooking the Bassin de Thau and the oyster beds of Bouzigues. Surrounding the abbey are 350 hectares of vineyards, of which 70 hectares are in production, all organically grown; the steepest parcels (40 hectares) were classified as AOC Coteaux du Languedoc in 1985. This site, with its remote location and natural spring, originally fulfilled all the conditions necessary for a Cistercian monastery. For 171 years now the d'Allaines family have lived in the private quarters at the southern end of the precinct. 'As a child, I took our way of life for granted,' recalls Madame d'Allaines. 'But time changed that, persuading me to open the abbey to the public in 1975. My mother objected at first but soon warmed to the idea when she realized it would help us sell our wines.' That year, for the first time in its rich history, Valmagne bottled wines under its own label – to the infinite chagrin of the *négociants* who previously bought the wine in barrels. Over the next 30 years the number of annual visitors would increase seventy-fold – from 400 in 1975 to some 30,000 in 2009. And what of the visitors themselves? Much more demanding than they used to be, says Diane, but also much more appreciative. 'Heritage in general has become infinitely more respectable.' A guided tour of this impeccably preserved estate is sure to win over even the most recalcitrant visitor.

Le secret de Frère Nonenque

Abbaye de Valmagne
Mis en bouteille à la propriété

Above: The label of the Vin de Pays that commemorates Frère Nonenque, cellar-master at Valmagne until his death in 1575. He died at the hands of his apostate abbot who fought on the Protestant Huguenot side in the French Wars of Religion.

Opposite: Vats in the nave of Valmagne Abbey church. The nave is twice as high as it is wide, the impression of height emphasized by the pointed arches, which are at their sharpest at the eastern end of the nave (the *chevet*) where the columns are closer together.

Left: The bell tower, restored between 1998 and 2000. Stripped of its bells in the French Revolution, it would be another 200 years before Valmagne's melodious chimes rang forth once again. The replaced bells were blessed by Jean Pierre Ricard, Bishop of Montpellier, on 29 April 2000.

Below, left: The cloister dates from the 13th century, rebuilt at the same time as the church. Four colonnaded walkways give onto the rooms in the oldest parts of the abbey (the chapter house, the parlour, the sacristy and the refectory). Numerology was a key aspect of medieval constructions: 'four' symbolizing wholeness, totality, completion (four cardinal points, four winds, four elements).

Opposite, above: Medieval Christians believed that the taller the church, the nearer it was to God. Valmagne Abbey church is 75 ft (23 m) high by 272 ft (83 m) long, inspired by the great cathedrals of northern France. Dubbed the 'cathedral of the vines' for its famous vats, it ranks as a classical example of Gothic architecture. Key features include the pointed arches, ribbed vaulting and flying buttresses.

Opposite, below: The cloister with the chapter house door at the far end. Glimpsed through the colonnade on the right is the black bamboo brought back from China by an intrepid d'Allaines ancestor – one of very few Europeans to visit the Forbidden Kingdom.

Left: Staircase in the family's private quarters, added by Madame d'Allaines some 30 years ago. The young man in the portrait is an ancestor on the Elbée side. The walls in this part of the abbey are 4 ft (1.2 m) thick. The private wing, like the inner courtyard, dates from the 17th century. It is believed to have been renovated by Florentine nobleman and Archbishop of Narbonne, Cardinal Pierre de Bonzi, who 'reigned' over Valmagne from 1680 to 1697.

Opposite, above, left: Bagheera, the abbey cat – a feline presence that has delighted visitors of all ages for the past 15 years.

Opposite, above, right: The lavabo-fountain in the cloister garden. The water pouring from these sculpted spouts comes from the spring of Diana, which has flowed since Roman times.

Opposite, below, left: Stained-glass window in the refectory – a rare treasure in an abbey that lost most of its stained glass during the French Wars of Religion in the 16th century.

Opposite, below, right: Valmagne's flagship *cuvées* are named after key figures in the abbey's history. This one, the Cuvée Comte de Turenne, commemorates Count Henri Amédée Mercure de Turenne (the grandfather of Madame d'Allaines' great-great-grandmother) who purchased the abbey in 1838 and saved it from destruction.

THE SOUTH-WEST

CHÂTEAU DE SAURS

Château de Saurs lies some 30 miles northeast of Toulouse and 12 miles west of Albi, at the south-easternmost tip of the winegrowing region termed 'South West France'. This represents an area of roughly 40,000 hectares covering everything south of Cognac and the Massif Central, except for Bordeaux, down to the foothills of the Pyrenees and the Spanish border, and extending eastwards into the department of the Tarn. There are some 30 appellations in all, with little in common beyond a predominantly oceanic (Atlantic) climate. Even the word for wine changes with the location: *ardantz* in Basque, *vinha* in Occitan. Château de Saurs stands at the point where Atlantic weather begins to give way to Mediterranean influences – a singular blessing in terms of climate and geography.

There have been Gineste de Saurs in the area for 600 years, making this one of the oldest estates in the Gaillac appellation. It is however a relative youngster compared to Gaillac as a whole, which is France's oldest winegrowing region (along with the Languedoc). Gaillac wines were regulated by royal charter as early as 1221, long before the present AOC system was even thought of. In more recent times, they were among the first to receive AOC classification. Hence the slogan of the Gaillac wine trade association: 'Wines with a future always have a past.' For Yves Burrus at Château de Saurs it's 'all about playing to your strengths – applying modern thinking to ancestral methods.' His wife Marie-Paule is the twentieth successive generation of Gineste de Saurs to own this estate. She is to the manner born, but husband Yves was and still is a banker (a scion of Switzerland's Burrus family of industrialists). His latest venture is micro-credit, prompted by his desire 'to share our good fortune with the world in need.'

Château de Saurs is indeed a privileged legacy. The house itself is a listed building, constructed between 1848 and 1852 for Marie-Paule's great-great-grandfather, Eliézer Gineste de Saurs. He himself was a Toulouse barrister of some repute – in sharp contrast to the allegedly illiterate architect of the semi-basement *chai* (wine cellar). The château stands on a hillside, screened by venerable pines and cypresses and flanked by vineyards at the front and back – 40 hectares of sloped plantings on the right bank of the River Tarn. All of the vines are organically grown and every parcel is separately vinified. Yves Burrus is a very 'hands on' proprietor, described by his sales manager Norbert de Caires as 'passionately involved from start to finish.' At the helm of this estate for more than 30 years now, Yves says he learned everything as he went along – 'supported, then and now, by people much more knowledgeable than myself.' His winemaking philosophy is as sensible and shrewd as you would expect of a seasoned banker: 'We are artisans of wine – too small to be big but with everything it takes to be special.'

Opposite: The north façade with its ancient wisteria, planted in 1872, and ornamental fishpond in the foreground. The house's cruciform, temple-like design is typically Palladian, affording fine views in all directions and combining beauty with the practical needs of a farmhouse. The *chai* occupies the entire semi-basement, with reception rooms and bedrooms above. The turkey in the foreground was made out of recycled oil drums by local sculptor Jean-Luc Favero.

Left: Wine label of Château de Saurs' Réserve Eliézer, based on an engraving of the château's south façade, and named in homage to the man who built this house in the mid-19th century, Toulouse barrister Eliézer Gineste de Saurs. The grapes, Braucol, Syrah and Merlot, are from selected parcels, with yields limited to 40 hectares so as to obtain perfectly ripe fruit, steeped in all the character of its *terroir*.

Opposite: View north from the house, looking down an alley of Parasol pines that are as old as the château itself. The trees reach up to 85 ft (26 m) high, their dense canopy spreading into the surrounding woodlands. On the left is the former stable wing, built some fifteen years after the house itself. The present stables, now home to polo ponies, are located far enough away for the smell to be no problem…

Right: Seen behind the wicker-covered flagon is the carved wooden headpiece destined to grace the entrance to the new tasting and visitor reception facilities.

Below: Real-life cock strutting on a cement planter bench on the north side of the property. The Burrus are keen animal lovers and there are chickens everywhere.

Above: The entrance to the former stable wing, with matching French doors facing east and south over the garden. This floor is now the orangery, where some 40 lemon trees spend the winter, with the fermenting room on the floor above. The doors are relatively recent additions, dating from the time of the conversion. The hunting trophies were bagged by Yves who says he has probably 'hunted in the four corners of the world.'

Opposite: The palatial entrance hall (65 x 50 ft, 20 x 15 m), featuring a full-length portrait of Eliézer Gineste de Saurs in hunting dress. The ceiling is 16 ft (5 m) high. The wrought-iron chandelier is of Italian origin, bought on impulse by the Burrus on the Quai Voltaire in Paris.

Left: Close-up of the kitchen fireplace with Moroccan bellows, a present from an employee who has been with the Burrus for 22 years.

Above: The kitchen, with two Portuguese high-back chairs against the wall.

Above: The *chai* provides the ideal environment for wine storage – to think that the man who built it could apparently neither read nor write… The smaller casks (225 litres) contain the Réserve Eliézer, the larger casks in the foreground hold the latest addition to the range, La Pigario. The wine is both fermented and aged in oak, always in these 400-litre barrels. For château winemaker Christian Alcouffe, La Pigario is a perfect example of modern thinking applied to ancestral methods: 'Cask fermentation has been around for centuries; but regulating the size of the casks, for instance, was our idea.'

Right: Selected wines from the Château de Saurs range. The grapes come from south-facing vineyards at the front and back of the house, protected from north winds by the slope. Harvesting is mechanical except for La Pigario and the *en primeur* red (both made from hand-picked fruit). The wines also benefit from a ready market: the Relais de l'Entrecôte restaurant chain, founded by Paul Gineste de Saurs and considerably expanded since by his daughter Marie-Paule, now with outlets in Paris, Geneva and Beirut.

CHÂTEAU DE BÉLINGARD

The owner of this estate is Count Laurent de Bosredon, an economist by training who returned to his winegrowing roots in the 1980s and has never looked back. Built in the 1850s by his great-great-grandfather Hippolyte Clauzel, Château de Bélingard was the lifelong home of his grandmother, Blanche de Bosredon. 'We used to call her "Bonne maman toute Blanche" – she was the heart and soul of this house,' recalls the Count. 'A remarkable woman – mother of eight, at the helm of this estate for nearly 60 years and fit as a fiddle until the day she died aged 103. Naturally, Bélingard wine had a lot to do with it.' Ambrosia of the Gods? The Ancient Druids certainly thought so. It was the Druids who named this site 'Bélingard', meaning 'Garden of the Sun God'. The Druids worshipped on this hilltop for thousands of years, and made sacred wine from the wild *vitis lambrusca* vines that once grew around the oak trees. It was believed that the hill stood on a ley line, at the meeting point of telluric energies that were harnessed in pagan rituals. To judge from the almost magical powers of the *Botrytis* fungus, those telluric forces are still at work today. *Botrytis cinerea* can be nasty or nice: it all depends on the mesoclimate and the grape variety. Grey rot is the unwelcome sort, caused by prolonged cool, wet weather that turns the crop to a mushy, grey mess. Noble Rot is what happens when damp, misty mornings give way to dry, sunny afternoons. In this respect, the vineyards of Château de Bélingard are truly blessed. Cradled between the Dordogne and Gardonette rivers, Sémillon, Muscadelle and Sauvignon vines ripen here to rotted perfection – shrivelled, intensely sweet and ideal for the making of Monbazillac wine.

The estate as we know it today was established in the 1940s by the present Count's father, Pierre de Bosredon, son of Blanche. Count Laurent took over as winemaker in 1988, armed with oenological qualifications but no practical experience to speak of. Three difficult formative years (storms, crop failure and frost damage) soon changed that. The vineyards he operates today are some of the finest and oldest in Monbazillac, combining traditional methods with state-of-the-art winemaking technology. The Count himself is disarmingly dismissive of his achievements. 'Somebody has to claim responsibility for the winemaking and it might as well be me. But, basically, I'm just the man who sweeps up after everyone else.' The house itself fares no better, described by the Count as a 'maison de notaire in the country', built by a 'fellow who was certainly no oil painting himself.' But he waxes lyrical about the view, with the vineyards of the Dordogne valley rolling away to the horizon. Reading between the lines, it is clear that the Count is a dedicated man, nurturing a legend that started with the Druids and continued with the Benedictine monks who settled here in the 7th century. Which of his wines does he prefer? The golden Monbazillac or the red, white and rosé Bergeracs? 'Can a parent have a favourite child?' he replies. Spoken like a true winemaker.

Opposite, above: The view reaches west for some 40 miles, all the way to Castillon-la-Bataille, scene of the very last battle of the Hundred Years War. Vestiges of Druidism are everywhere – such as the magnificent oaks pictured here. 'But contrary to popular legend,' claims the Count, 'it was not mistletoe that the Druids cut down from the oak trees but wild grapes.'

Right: Sémillon vineyards extend westwards, accounting for 60 per cent of total plantings (roughly 80 hectares under vine).

Opposite: The entrance hall, featuring the 'horribly awkward' spiral staircase that winds its way up to the second floor (with only the loft beyond). The chandelier (centre) dates from the 19th century and originally hung beneath a garden canopy outdoors, 'a reminder of our "Creole" connections,' explains the Count. The family spent 200 years in Guadeloupe and Martinique, only returning to France in the 19th century. Famous forebears include Gilles de Rey (1404–40) more commonly called 'Blue Beard'; and Dr Joseph Ignace Guillotin (1738–1814), advocate (but not the inventor) of the guillotine.

Right: The dining room, featuring a painting by an artist friend whose works were exhibited at the château. 'The painting was a gift from my wife Sylvie – it's how she expects me to look when I retire…' Seen on the dresser is the bell used by Blanche de Bosredon to summon her lady companion – rung by visiting relatives ever since as a nostalgic reminder of their grandmother. The wine is a double magnum of Vin Rouge de Bélingard.

Opposite, above: The dining room is 1,700 sq ft (50 sq m) and some 29 ft (9 m) long. At harvest time, the table is extended on trestles and runs the length of the room. Some 25 people (full-time staff only) eat lunch here throughout the harvest period, including the Count and Countess. The wines are Bélingard reds, served sparingly since there are tractors to drive after lunch.

Opposite, below: Pictured below left is a bottle of the Cuvée Blanche de Bosredon, created by the Count in 1988 in memory of his beloved grandmother who died that same year. The glass with the twisted stem was designed that way. The apples (below, right) are from the Count's own orchard, which is planted with some 50 ancestral species. 'What could be nicer,' he asks, 'than a freshly picked apple straight from the tree?'

Right: The huge family kitchen (1,000 sq ft, 31 sq m) with the 'débotté' in the foreground (literally the 'debooting area'). The high chair against the wall (like the toddler's chair at the foot of the spiral staircase – see preceding pages) are part of a small collection belonging to the Countess. The floor, here and in the hallway, is original and typical of the period. The baroque chandelier in the kitchen, so daringly out of place in these surroundings, is characteristic of a delightfully eclectic mix of furniture that perfectly embodies the Count's witty eccentricity.

Above: The 'petit salon' (aka family room or den). On the right is a portrait of Alexandre de Bosredon, the Count's great-great-grand uncle. The parquet floor dates from the 1950s, what the Count calls a 'less-than-lovely' reminder of an outbreak of *la mérule* (dry rot).

Right: Bronze figurine (possibly inspired by Joan of Arc) by the 18th-century French artist Pierre-Paul Prud'hon. The portraits are, top left, the Count's great-uncle, brother of the Count's grandfather (with whom he was always on bad terms); and below and right, two lady ancestors on the Clauzel side of the family. The great-uncle died without issue and, determined not to leave anything to his brother, he left it instead to his brother's eight children. Each spent his inheritance according to his tastes – the Count's father bought a tractor.

Opposite: The 'salon de réception', where visitors get a taste of dynastic tradition. On the table is a genealogical record of the de Bosredon family traced back to 1180.

BORDEAUX

CHÂTEAU BATAILLEY

The master of this estate is Philippe Casteja, who was born in the château and spent most of his youth here – except for a few years at prep school and public school in England. Speaking English was the custom in the Casteja family, whose roots in Pauillac date back to the early 1600s. Bordeaux was a British possession for nearly three centuries and, as Philippe wryly points out, it was the English flag that his ancestors fought under in the Hundred Years War. These very vineyards, between Pauillac and Saint-Julien, are said to have been the site of England's last-ditch attempt to retain Aquitaine – hence the name 'Batailley', suggesting a battle or military skirmish. Looking around the area today, it is hard to believe the British ever left. The Dordogne in northwest Aquitaine even has its own cricket team…

The house and vineyard are of a piece, unchanged since the 19th century. The vineyard, in particular, is exceptionally homogeneous, with no major replanting since 1855 (the year that Batailley entered the first official classification of Bordeaux wines). 'This is one of the few Médoc vineyards that has always been well maintained – dependable year after year, with no rough patches,' says Philippe. At the helm since 2001, he is scrupulously reticent about his own, much-acclaimed achievements, claiming only to have done 'at least as well' as his father, Emile.

The house itself is a traditional Médoc property, in the best neo-classical tradition. Built in the late 1700s, it was enlarged and modified thereafter, acquiring its present style in the 1850s. Laid out around five courtyards, the property is home to an immense hangar-like structure that was originally constructed for the Paris Exposition Universelle of 1889 – the trade fair that saw the unveiling of the Eiffel Tower. Philippe says he has no idea how the structure got here –

CHATEAU BATAILLEY
GRAND CRU CLASSÉ
PAUILLAC

only that it can house up to 500 people at a time. 'These courtyards used to bustle with activity at harvest time. As a child, I used to love watching the women prepare meals in the "cuisines de vendanges" [harvest kitchens]. Delicious smells wafting through the air … huge, steaming cauldrons of split-pea soup, enough for all the pickers and their families.' All of Batailley's grapes are still picked by hand, but the harvest kitchens and everything that went with them are now long gone.

The historic soul of the house lives on, however, lovingly preserved by Philippe's parents, Emile and Denise. The château has been their home for more than 50 years and, however grandiose the exterior may be, it feels very warm and lived in on the inside. This is the eternal inheritance that will pass to Philippe's eldest son, Frédéric, who now works alongside his father. Philippe's nephew, Peer Pfeiffer, has also joined the family business. 'For any parent,' concludes Philippe, 'it is surely gratifying to know that the historic traditions of a family property such as this will continue in the hands of the children.'

Above: The château today – essentially unchanged since 1850 (witness the etching on the left). The gardens are the work of gifted 19th-century French horticulturist Jean-Pierre Barillet-Deschamps, best known as the designer of the Jardin Vauban in Lille, for Empress Eugénie. Barillet-Deschamps was much in demand for his 'picturesque' use of sub-tropical bedding plants – such as the wild cyclamen that grace these grounds in late summer. A touch of delicacy that works wonders in this gracious but imposing setting.

Opposite: A bibliophile's playground, the Batailley library is lined with books from floor to ceiling. Rare titles, hand-bound editions, complete works – bibliophilic treasures spill over into the adjoining corridors, testifying to Emile Casteja's lifelong love of literature. 'This is still my father's favourite room,' says Philippe Casteja. 'And the place where my sister and I spent many happy hours as children. There would always be music playing (anything from Bach to Johnny Hallyday) and a fire burning in the hearth.' Note that the cellar is as well stocked as the library, boasting more than 50,000 bottles of wine from Batailley's own vineyards. Food for the intellect and food for the senses…

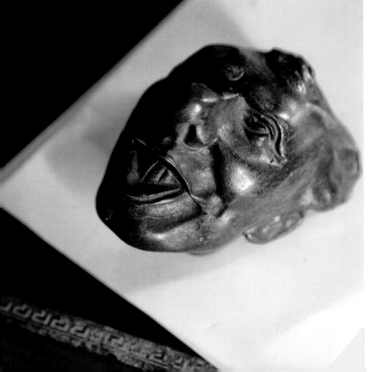

Left and above: The house is richly furnished with family heirlooms and antiques. 'Every knick-knack, painting and piece of furniture has a story,' says Philippe Casteja. The interior decoration is predominantly 18th century, but with assorted memorabilia added over the decades – such as the classical statuette pictured above and intriguing mask (left), in the Grotesque style.

CHÂTEAU DU TAILLAN

In the beginning, the French term 'bourgeois' signified a citizen of a 'bourg' or market town, especially one beside a castle (from the Latin *burgus*, castle). Over the centuries the term came to define the affluent middle classes – merchants, professionals and gentlemen farmers – as distinct from the nobles at the top of the scale and the peasants at the bottom. The title 'cru bourgeois' first appeared in the 15th century, meaning a Bordeaux wine estate with a middle-class proprietor.

Château du Taillan is a Cru Bourgeois, one of 247 châteaux, all in the Médoc, that make up the Cru Bourgeois classification. In 1896 the estate was acquired by prosperous wine merchant, Henri Cruse, some 80 years after his forebear Hermann first arrived in Bordeaux from the family's native Schleswig-Holstein. It was customary in those days for young middle-class men to be sent abroad to learn a trade. In Bordeaux they did better than that – they created one. The wines shipped back to Germany by Hermann and his contemporaries laid the foundations of what is today the single largest export market for Bordeaux wines. The château's present managing director is Armelle Falcy-Cruse, one of five sisters with three daughters of her own. 'Château Taillan remained a father-to-son holding for nearly 100 years – until no son came along and I stepped in.' What Armelle brings to the table is all the same true to Cruse tradition: a shrewd business sense and a healthy appetite for opportunity, mainly in the form of wine tourism. Her approach to the management of this 100 hectare estate is resolutely forward looking, inspired by her years in the Napa Valley. 'Historic monuments are all very fine but they must not become stuck in the past.' There seems little danger of that here. The house remains delightfully unspoilt, a family home then and now, with that patina of humanity that accumulates over time. Moviemakers love it as the romantic setting for period dramas. So too do wedding couples, who seal their vows in the chiaroscuro atmosphere of 16th-century *chais* once occupied by the Knights Templar.

There are gourmet picnics in the grounds – oysters *à l'ancienne* in the literal sense – and *table d'hôte* dinners with Armelle and her husband, *la vie de château* on a plate – a deceptively effortless performance. It isn't easy juggling the needs of a family home that is also a business asset, especially when the property in question happens to be located in a bastion of traditionalism like the Médoc. But Armelle obviously welcomes the challenge. 'Call me avant-garde, but I think it's high time we demystified all the ceremony surrounding wine – show people that serving wine doesn't have to be a headache. You don't need a tie and white gloves to enjoy Château du Taillan.'

Above: Former wine label (replaced in 1997) designed by keen horseman, the late Henri-François Cruse. The horses shown here are now long gone but the stables remain, opening up a host of business possibilities.

Opposite: The white stone façade is pure 18th century, a rebuilding following a fire. The oldest part of the house (left) is 16th century and features a water tower that originally supplied the whole building. The 'veranda' connecting the two parts of the house is 19th century, added by Henri Cruse in around 1896 along with the roof balustrade. Pictured in the foreground is the vineyard, separated from the grounds by a terrace: 30 hectares of vines in production, planted in a single east-facing block.

Below: Close-up of the terrace (also pictured on the preceding pages), with fabulous views a mile into the distance.

Right: The Virginia Creeper-clad walls of the 16th-century wing, flanked by two statues, two of many added by Henri Cruse in the late 1800s. This part of the house is now occupied by Armelle's mother, while Armelle and family occupy private quarters in the main house.

Left: The 'salon rond' ('round' reception room) where aperitifs and morning coffee are served, looking through to the 'salon carré' ('square' reception room) and the dining room, with the veranda beyond. The door just visible in the foreground leads into the 'grand salon' (main reception room). The furnishings are as eclectic as you would expect of a house that has remained a family home since 1896.

Opposite: The grand entrance, with elegant stone staircase and handsome wrought-iron balustrade. Seen on the landing is a French *trumeau* mirror (a mirror and painting in one). The window faces west, onto the courtyard.

Opposite: The atmospheric 16th-century *chai*, with a bust of the 'Dame Blanche' in the foreground. Added by Armelle's father, its presence enhances the magic of these surroundings. When local people refer to the 'Dame Blanche' they mean the mist that settles on the vines in early autumn – said to bring good luck to those who see it. She has certainly brought good luck to the Cruse family: their white wine, called 'Dame Blanche' is regularly sold out. It is of course labelled 'Bordeaux Blanc' and not 'Médoc' (there being no such thing as a white Médoc).

Right: The 'grand salon' (as glimpsed on the preceding pages). The wood panelling is early 19th century, added by the inexhaustible Henri Cruse (a man with an appetite for 'Herculean works', according to Armelle). Against the wall is a cylinder desk; the screen to its left is a classical example of 'bric-à-brac' added over the generations.

CHÂTEAU DE ROZIER

The story of Château Rozier begins with Jean Saby, a winegrower who left his native Massif Central in the 1770s and bought a small plot of vines near the town of Saint Emilion, on the right bank of the Gironde River. He settled in the village of Saint-Laurent-des-Combes, some five miles from Libourne, in the province of Guyenne (now the department of the Gironde). Eventually he built a house – this house – using locally quarried *calcaire à astéries* (starfish limestone). *Calcaire à astéries* is to the Gironde what chalk is to Champagne: the mark of the region's architecture and its wines. Saint Emilion is built on it, as too is Bordeaux – hence its other name, 'pierre de Bordeaux'.

Over the years, this style of house became known as a 'Girondine', a house typical of the area and winegrowers like Jean Saby: smallholders from peasant backgrounds who were winegrowers and also stone masons. 'The Gironde has thousands of houses like this one,' says Jean-Philippe Saby, who runs the estate today with his brother Jean-Christophe and father Jean-Bernard. 'And they always face due south, whatever the lie of the land.' The house follows the classical 'Girondine' format of a plain rectangular main building with two lower side extensions – what he calls the 'ears' – at the western and eastern ends. These were invariably added later, by subsequent generations with higher expectations of comfort. In this case, they house the kitchen and the office. A particular feature that marks this house out as a winegrower's house is the location of the *chai* (winery proper). This is always a single-storey building, attached to the house on its northern side with cool conditions in mind. 'Wine doesn't mind the cold,' says Jean-Philippe. 'It's heat that's the problem – not forgetting all the heat generated by fermentation.'

When Jean Saby settled here nearly 250 years ago, Saint Emilion was a remote rural area on the Bordeaux Right Bank, cut off from the city itself by two major rivers. It would be at least another 40 years before there was a bridge across the Dordogne at Libourne or across the Garonne at Bordeaux. Yet all of his descendants followed him into the business, gradually piecing together what is today a 25 hectare holding in the Saint Emilion Grand Cru appellation.

Jean-Philippe and his brother have never considered any other life – winemaking flows through their veins, he says. 'Our family is rooted in this house. My brother and I know we will always make Château Rozier because what we extract from each plot says more about our family history than the vineyard itself.' And with such a mosaic-like variety of plots to play with, added by successive generations of Sabys, what they produce in the end is a wine greater than the sum of its parts – 'a wine with an identity all of its own.'

'Round here, we have a saying,' says Jean-Philippe, '"On fait la vigne" – meaning that for us our vines are like children. We plant them, we raise them and care for them for 100–150 years, and we stand by them until the end of their natural lives.'

Opposite: The property faces due south, looking out over roughly half a hectare of grounds. The roof is clad in *tuiles à côte de Marseille* (flat interlocking clay roof tiles) – 'a far cry from the lovely "tuiles canals" [barrel roof tiles] boasted by Saint Emilion,' sighs Jean-Philippe.

Overleaf, left: The dining room on the south side of the house. The furnishings are French Empire style, and the floor is French *point d'Hongrie* parquet (solid oak floorboards). Pictured on the right, behind the open door, is a 16th-century relief ceramic of grape harvesting.

Overleaf, right page, above: The world heritage site of Saint Emilion, viewed from the foot of the spire that stands above Europe's largest underground monolithic church. Beneath the church is a hermit's cell carved out of the rock by the town's founder, an 8th-century monk and travelling confessor called Aemilianus.

Overleaf, right page, below, left: Château de Rozier (85% Merlot and 15% Cabernet Franc) and Château Hauchat (100% Merlot, from the Sabys' Fronsac holding).

Overleaf, right page, below, right: Oval-shaped Napoleon III marquetry table, with a floral patterned exotic wood veneer and cambered base in dark brown pearwood.

Left: The main entrance, featuring the magnificent elm wood staircase – a precious relic from the days before Dutch elm disease. The hunting horn in the foreground belonged to Jean-Philippe's grandfather, the first in his family who was not also a stonemason. Jean-Philippe's three-year-old son Paul is meanwhile the first male descendant not to have been christened 'Jean', which is not to deny the strong sense of dynastic continuity that drives this family.

Opposite: The children's bedroom, occupied by generations of budding winegrowers. Jean-Philippe's own children, Agathe (aged six) and Paul, still sleep here today when staying with their great-grandparents. The wallpaper dates from the days when this was their grandfather Jean-Bernard's bedroom. The stove in the fireplace, once the only source of heating in this room, is now in retirement thanks to central heating.

CHÂTEAU LAFITE ROTHSCHILD

Château Lafite Rothschild was ranked 'Premier des Premiers Crus', leader among fine wines, when the wines of France were first classified for the 1855 Exposition Universelle de Paris. That position remains unchallenged today, zealously guarded by five generations of French Rothschilds, ever since Baron James Mayer de Rothschild first acquired the property in 1868. Lafite Rothschild still ranks top of only five First Growths, now the glittering jewel in the crown of its parent company, Domaines Barons de Rothschild (DBR). Presiding over it all is Baron Eric de Rothschild whose 35-year tenure at Lafite has produced a sumptuous portfolio of holdings in France and across the world.

The property lies at the northern end of the Pauillac appellation, some 35 miles from the city of Bordeaux. This is the cream of the Bordeaux Left Bank, home of a star-studded line-up of châteaux. Château Lafite Rothschild is surprisingly relaxed by comparison, displaying a pleasurable mixture of styles that Baron Eric describes as a 'hotch potch'. Originally the seat of a medieval seigneury, all that remains of the old building is a fairytale turret that dates back to the 16th century. The two-storey château is 18th century, the outbuildings 19th century and the circular, second-year concrete *chai* – the first circular ageing cellar anywhere in the world – is late 20th century.

Despite (or perhaps because of) its mixed architectural parentage, the château creates a strikingly harmonious effect – 'just like the wine it celebrates,' says Baron Eric. 'After the second or third glass you realize that it's a wine which has all the subtlety and all the qualities… I always say it's the difference between a one-night stand and the girl you marry. You want to marry Lafite.'

Madame de Pompadour would no doubt have agreed with him: she adored Lafite, as presumably did her lover, Louis XV, who elevated Lafite's owner, Nicolas-Alexandre de Ségur, to the rank of marquis (who became known in his lifetime as the 'Prince of Vines'). English statesman Sir Robert Walpole bought the 1732 and 1733 vintages in barrel. Father of the American Declaration of Independence, Thomas Jefferson, was another lifelong admirer of Lafite. More recently, Hermann Goering, the notorious Nazi general, is said to have had designs on Lafite – which was saved from German clutches only by being expropriated by the Vichy Government.

By the 19th century Lafite boasted some 75 hectares in production and was sold at auction – lock, stock and barrel – for a cool 5 million francs. The buyer was Baron James Mayer Rothschild, great-great-grandfather of Baron Eric, who describes himself as 'the first really hands-on owner. Even Ségur had a *régisseur*.' Lafite remains an estate of superlatives. Over 100 hectares of ultra-poor, gravel and sand soils produce what is widely regarded as the finest wine in the world. Only Lafite makes all of its barrels in its own house cooperage, and only Lafite combines remarkably traditional winemaking with the most modern wine-maturation facility in the Médoc. The most expensive wine ever sold was a Lafite: in 1985 the 1787 Lafite sold at single-bottle auction for US$156,000, a record that remains unsurpassed today.

Above: Château Lafite Rothschild is set in manicured grounds, each plant impeccably shaped, each tree pruned to perfection. The major part of the vineyard lies adjacent to the château building, on deep beds of gravel and Aeolian sand underpinned by limestone. The average age of the vines is 40 years, the oldest being about 90 years. Vines aged 80 years plus are (reluctantly) replaced with new stock (roughly one per cent of replanting per annum). The Cabernet Sauvignon represents 70% of plantings, supported by the Merlot (25%), Cabernet France (3%) and Petit Verdot (2%).

Left: The 'salon rouge' (red room): this is the reception room where aperitifs are served before lunch or dinner. The portrait on the wall is of pianist, water-colourist and collector Baroness Nathaniel de Rothschild, née Charlotte de Rothschild (1825–99) to whom Frédéric Chopin, her piano teacher, dedicated one of his Opus 69 waltzes. It was Nathaniel de Rothschild (1812–70) who founded the French winemaking branch of the Rothschild family, purchasing the neighbouring Pauillac estate, Château Brane-Mouton, in 1853 (now Mouton-Rothschild). Two years later, when Mouton was ranked a Second Growth in the Bordeaux Wine Classification of 1855, a disappointed Nathaniel gave the following response: 'Premier ne puis, second ne daigne, Mouton suis' (First I cannot be, second I will not deign to be, Mouton I am).

Opposite, above: The 'red room' looking decidedly red, with richly upholstered sofas and *bergères*, faithful to the Second Empire style of Napoleon III and lavishly furnished with silks and brocades. The château has an ornately classical look, helped by a pleasing play of light and shadow as the sun moves across the sky. Every room in the château comes into its own at a certain hour, says Baron Eric. 'The yellow room in the morning; the red room before lunch; the green room at night.'

Right: Close-up of a *chinoiserie* chest, heavily encrusted with mother-of-pearl inlay and topped by a decorative round box made of pink glass with a grape motif.

Overleaf: The grand piano in the 'red room', laden with family portraits of past generations.

Opposite: The 'salon vert' (green room): the drawing room where guests adjourn after dining for coffee, *digestifs* and cigars.

Right: Small portrait of Betty de Rothschild (1805–86), wife of Baron James Mayer de Rothschild (1792–1868), who was the original purchaser of the château in 1868 – 15 years after his nephew Nathaniel de Rothschild purchased Château Brane-Mouton next door. The Baron died just three months later, mourned by thousands according to Nathaniel. Betty's portrait stands on a desk in the 'red room', a fine example of the classical portrait style – in mischievous contrast to the highly ornamented and coloured rococo candlestick in the foreground.

Above: A portrait of Baron Edmond de Rothschild (1845–1934), a famous philanthropist, painted by the French artist Aimé Morot.

Right: Lafite's innovative, circular second-year aging cellar has space for 2,200 barrels. 'As soon as you did your homework,' explains Baron Eric, 'you realized it had to be round. Long *chais*, though traditional, were nonsense from the point of view of efficiency. A round *chai* meant columns, and columns meant Ricardo Bofill, a personal friend of mine whose sense of space I have always much admired. He wasn't used to having somebody work so closely with him, but he took the job knowing that it had to be round.'

WINE ESTATES BY REGION

The Loire Valley

1 Château de Vaugaudry
2 Château de Brissac
3 Château de Coulaine
4 Château de Tracy

Champagne

5 Roederer
6 Taittinger
7 Bollinger

Alsace

8 Domaine Schlumberger
9 Domaine Weinbach

Burgundy

10 Château de Chorey-les-Beaune
11 Château de Béru
12 Château Fuissé
13 Château des Péthières

Jura

14 Château d'Arlay

Savoie

15 Domaine de Méjane

The Rhône Valley

16 Jean-Louis Chave
17 Domaine de l'Oratoire Saint Martin
18 Château Fortia

Provence

19 Château de Saint Martin
20 Château Vannières
21 Mas de la Dame

Corsica

22 Clos Capitoro

Languedoc-Roussillon

23 Château de Jau
24 Château de Pennautier
25 Abbaye de Valmagne

The South-West

26 Château de Saurs
27 Château de Bélingard

Bordeaux

28 Château Batailley
29 Château du Taillan
30 Château de Rozier
31 Château Lafite Rothschild

ENGLISH CHANNEL

BELGIUM

LUXEMBOURG

GERMANY

Lille

Amiens

Cherbourg

Le Havre

Rouen

Caen

Metz

Strasbourg

5

Reims

7

Épernay

Châlons-en-
Champagne

6

CHAMPAGNE

Paris

ALSACE

9

Colmar

Troyes

Bar-sur-Aube

Bar-sur-Seine

8

Mulhouse

Auxerre

11

Tonnerre

Vendôme

Orléans

Rennes

Brest

St-Nazaire

Ancenis

Angers

Tours

Blois

Sancerre

4

Dijon

Nantes

2

Cholet

3

Chinon

Reuilly

Pouilly-sur-Loire

LOIRE VALLEY

1

Thouars

Bourges

BURGUNDY

Beaune

10

14

Arbois

Chalon-
sur-Saône

JURA

SWITZERLAND

Poitiers

Châteaumeillant

Mâcon

BEAUJOLAIS

12

La Rochelle

13

Villefranche

SAVOIE

ATLANTIC
OCEAN

Limoges

Clermont-
Ferrand

Lyon

Chambéry

Vienne

15

St-Étienne

16

ITALY

Périgueux

31

28

30

29

Bordeaux

Bergerac

Valence

RHÔNE VALLEY

BORDEAUX

27

Langon

Cahors

MASSIF
CENTRAL

17

Orange

Agen

18

Avignon

SOUTH-WEST

Montauban

26

Albi

Nîmes

21

Nice

Auch

Toulouse

Montpellier

Aix

Cannes

Bayonne

25

Béziers

PROVENCE

19

St-Tropez

Pau

24

Carcassonne

Marseille

20

Toulon

**LANGUEDOC-
ROUSSILLON**

23

Perpignan

MEDITERRANEAN
SEA

SPAIN

ANDORRA

PYRENEES

ALPS

N

| 0 km | 50 | 100 | 150 | 200 |

| 0 miles | 50 | 100 |

CORSICA

Bastia

CORSICA

Ajaccio

22

Bonifacio

DIRECTORY

KEY   WHITE   ROSÉ   RED   SWEET   SPARKLING WHITE   SPARKLING ROSÉ   SPARKLING RED

The information given here is for guidance only. For further details or to arrange
a visit, please contact the property directly by phone or by email

THE LOIRE VALLEY

CHÂTEAU DE VAUGAUDRY

37500 Chinon
T 02 47 93 13 51
F 02 47 93 23 08
e chateau-de-vaugaudry@
wanadoo.fr
w www.chinon.com/vignoble/
chateau-vaugaudry

The cellars are open to visitors
all year round by appointment only

WINES

Château de Vaugaudry Rosé

Château de Vaugaudry
Château de Vaugaudry,
Clos du Plessis-Gerbault

CHÂTEAU DE BRISSAC

49320 Brissac
T 02 41 91 22 21
F 02 41 91 25 60
e chateau-brissac@wanadoo.fr
w www.chateau-brissac.fr

Bed and breakfast
accommodation

WINES

AOC Rosé d'Anjou

AOC Anjou
AOC Anjou Villages Brissac

CHÂTEAU DE COULAINE

37420 Beaumont en Véron
T 02 47 98 44 51
F 02 47 93 49 15
w www.chinon.com/vignoble/
chateau-coulaine

Wine tastings by appointment
only, please contact Etienne and
Pascale Bonnaventures:
T 02 47 98 44 51

For information about
chambres d'hôte at the château,
please contact Catherine de
Bonnaventure or Isabelle de
Kerros: **T** 02 47 81 20 07 /
06 08 84 63 05

WINES

Château de Coulaine Chinon

Bonnaventure Bourgueil
Bonnaventure Chinon
Château de Coulaine Bourgueil
Château de Coulaine Chinon
Château de Coulaine Touraine

Clos de Turpenay Chinon
Les Picasses Chinon
Les Pieds Rôtis Touraine

CHÂTEAU DE TRACY

58150 Pouilly-sur-Loire
T 03 86 26 15 12
F 03 86 26 10 73
w www.chateau-de-tracy.com

WINES

Château de Tracy Cuvée 101
Rangs Silex Pouilly-Fumé
Blanc
Château de Tracy Haute
Densité Pouilly-Fumé
Château de Tracy
'Mademoiselle de T'
Pouilly Fumé Blanc
Château de Tracy Pouilly
Fumé Blanc

CHAMPAGNE

ROEDERER

21 Boulevard Lundy, BP 66
51053 Reims
T 03 26 40 42 11
F 03 26 61 40 35
w www.champagne-roederer.
com

ⓘ Visits to the cellars are for professionals only

WINES

Blanc de Blancs
Brut Premier
Carte Blanche Demi Sec
Carte Blanche Extra Dry
Carte Blanche Sec
Cristal
Vintage Brut

Brut Rosé
Cristal Rosé
Rosé Vintage

TAITTINGER

9 Place Saint-Nicaise
51100 Reims
T 03 26 85 45 35
F 03 26 50 14 30
w www.taittinger.com

ⓘ Cellar tours every day, including Sundays and bank holidays, from mid-March to mid-November, from 9.30 am to 1 pm and from 2 pm to 5.30 pm (last tours at 12 noon and 4.30 pm); from mid-November to mid-March, Monday to Friday (closed on bank holidays)

WINES

Comtes de Champagne Blanc
   de Blancs
Cuvée Brut Millésimé
Cuvée Brut Réserve

Cuvée Folies de la
   Marquetterie
Cuvée Nocturne
Cuvée Prélude 'Grands Crus'

Comtes de Champagne Rosé
Cuvée Prestige Rosé

BOLLINGER

Office:
20 boulevard du Maréchal de
   Lattre de Tassigny
51160 Aÿ
T 03 26 53 33 66
F 03 26 54 85 59
w www.champagne-bollinger.fr

ⓘ To arrange a visit, please contact Pascale Pétry: p.petry@champagne-bollinger.fr

La Grande Année, Brut
   Vintage Champagne
Spéciale Cuvée, Brut NV
   Champagne
Vieilles Vignes Françaises,
   Blanc de Noirs Champagne

Brut Rosé NV Champagne
La Grande Année, Brut Rosé
   Champagne

Bollinger Coteaux Champenois
   'La Côte aux Enfants'

ALSACE

DOMAINE SCHLUMBERGER

100 rue Théodore Deck
68501 Guebwiller Cedex
T 03 89 74 27 00
F 03 89 74 85 75
w www.domaines-schlumberger.
   com

ⓘ The cellars are open from Monday to Thursday, from 8 am to 6 pm and on Fridays, from 8 am to 5 pm; closed at weekends

WINES

Les Princes Abbés

Grands Crus wines:
Grand Cru Kessler
Grand Cru Kitterlé
Grand Cru Saering
Grand Cru Spiegel

Schlumberger 'Collection':
Cuvée Anne: Gewurztraminer
   Sélection de Grains Nobles
Cuvée Christine:
   Gewurztraminer Vendanges
   Tardives
Cuvée Clarisse: Pinot Gris
   Sélection de Grains Nobles
Cuvée Ernest: Riesling,
   Sélection de Grains Nobles

Les Princes Abbés

Les Princes Abbés

DOMAINE WEINBACH

Clos des Capucins
25 Route du Vin
68240 Kaysersberg
T 03 89 47 13 21
F 03 89 47 38 18
w www.domaineweinbach.com

🕐 The cellars are open all year round except on Sundays and bank holidays

WINES

🍾 *'Réserve' selection*:
Muscat Réserve
Pinot Blanc Réserve

'Cuvée' and 'single-vineyard' ('lieu-dit') wines:
Gewurztraminer Altenbourg
Gewurztraminer Cuvée Laurence
Gewurztraminer Cuvée Théo
Pinot Gris Altenbourg
Pinot Gris Cuvée Sainte Catherine
Riesling Cuvée Sainte Catherine
Riesling Cuvée Théo

Grands Crus:
Gewurztraminer Grand Cru Furstentum
Gewurztraminer Grand Cru Mambourg
Riesling Grand Cru Schlossberg
Riesling Grand Cru Schlossberg Cuvée Sainte Catherine
Riesling Grand Cru Schlossberg Cuvée Sainte Catherine 'L'Inédit'

Late Harvest bottlings:
Gewurztraminer Altenbourg Vendanges Tardives
Gewurztraminer Grand Cru Furstentum Vendanges Tardives
Pinot Gris Altenbourg Vendanges Tardives
Riesling Grand Cru Schlossberg Vendanges Tardives

Gewurztraminer Altenbourg Sélection de Grains Nobles
Gewurztraminer Grand Cru Furstentum Sélection de Grains Nobles
Gewurztraminer Grand Cru Mambourg Sélection de Grains Nobles
Pinot Gris Altenbourg Sélection de Grains Nobles
Riesling Grand Cru Schlossberg Sélection de Grains Nobles

Gewurztraminer Grand Cru Mambourg Quintessence de Grains Nobles
Pinot Gris Altenbourg Quintessence de Grains Nobles
Riesling Grand Cru Schlossberg Quintessence de Grains Nobles

🍾 *'Réserve' selection:*
Pinot Noir Réserve
Sylvaner Réserve

BURGUNDY

CHÂTEAU DE CHOREY-LES-BEAUNE

2 Rue Jacques Germain
21200 Chorey-les-Beaune
T 03 80 22 06 05
F 03 80 24 03 93
e contact@chateau-de-chorey-les-beaune.fr
w www.chateau-de-chorey-les-beaune.fr

🛏 There are a number of rooms that can be reserved online from Easter to the end of October

🕐 The château is open from 1 July to 31 August, from 9 am to 11.30 am and from 2 pm to 5.30 pm. Entry to the park is free

WINES

🍾 Domaine de Château de Chorey Germain Beaune Premier Cru Cuvée Tante Berthe
Domaine de Château de Chorey Germain Beaune Premier Cru sur les Grèves
Domaine de Château de Chorey Germain Bourgogne

Domaine de Château de
   Chorey Germain Meursault
   les Pellans
Domaine de Château de
   Chorey Germain Pernand
   Vergelesses les Combottes

🍾 Domaine de Château de
   Chorey Germain Beaune
   Premier Cru Domaine
   de Saux
Domaine de Château de
   Chorey Germain Beaune
   Premier Cru les Cras
Domaine de Château de
   Chorey Germain Beaune
   Premier Cru les Teurons
Domaine de Château de
   Chorey Germain Beaune
   Premier Cru les Vignes
   Franches
Domaine de Château de
   Chorey Germain Bourgogne
Domaine de Château de
   Chorey Germain Bourgogne
   Premier Cru Cuvée
   Tante Berthe
Domaine de Château de
   Chorey Germain Chorey
   les Beaune

CHÂTEAU DE BÉRU

32 Grande Rue
89700 Béru
T 03 86 75 90 43
F 03 86 75 94 95
e contact@chateaudeberu.com
w www.chateaudeberu.com

🛏 There are three guest rooms

🕐ℹ Guided tours take place from
April to October, from 10.30 am
to 12 noon and from 3 pm to
6.30 pm, and by appointment
only from November to March.
Please email at other times
to arrange a visit

WINES

🍾 Chablis
   Chablis Clos Béru Monopole
   Chablis Premier Cru
   Vaucoupin

CHÂTEAU FUISSÉ

71960 Fuissé
T 03 85 35 61 44
F 03 3 85 35 67 34
w www.chateau-fuisse.fr

🕐ℹ Sales and tastings take place
in the château from Monday
to Friday, from 10 am to 12
noon and from 2 pm to 4 pm.
To visit at weekends, holidays
and bank holidays, please contact
the château

WINES

🍾 Pouilly-Fuissé Château-Fuissé
   Le Clos
   Pouilly-Fuissé Château-Fuissé
   Les Brûlés
   Pouilly Fuissé Château-Fuissé
   Les Combettes
   Pouilly-Fuissé Château-Fuissé
   Tête de Cru
   Saint Véran Château-Fuissé

Jean-Jacques Vincent et Fils wines
White Mâconnais wines:
Mâcon Fuissé
Mâcon Villages Champ Brûlé
Pouilly-Fuissé Marie Antoinette
Saint Véran Les Morats

White Burgundy wines:
Bourgogne Blanc JJ Vincent
Crémant de Bourgogne

🍾 *Red Beaujolais wines:*
Fleurie
Juliénas Le Cotoyon
Morgon Charmes

CHÂTEAU DES PÉTHIÈRES

69460 Saint-Etienne-des
   Ouillières
T 04 74 03 42 41 / 04 74 69 86 50
F 04 74 03 41 41 / 04 74 69 86 54
e guydelaperriere@gmail.com

WINES

🍾 Château des Péthières
   Beaujolais 'de garde'
   Château des Péthières
   Beaujolais Nouveau
   Château des Péthières Brouilly

JURA

CHÂTEAU D'ARLAY

Route de Saint-Germain
39140 Arlay
T 03 84 85 04 22
F 03 84 48 17 96
e chateau@arlay.com
w www.arlay.com

The cellars are open from
Monday to Friday, 9 am to
12 noon and from 2 pm to 6 pm;
on Saturdays from 9 am to 12 noon
and from 2 pm to 5 pm; closed
on Sundays and bank holidays.
The château, the gardens and
the park are open from the first
Saturday in June to the 3rd
Sunday in September, from
2 pm to 6 pm. Groups are
welcome by prior arrangement

WINES

Château d'Arlay 'à la Reine'
Château d'Arlay Straw Wine
Château d'Arlay White Macvin
Château d'Arlay White
    Tradition
Château d'Arlay Yellow Wine

Château d'Arlay Corail
Château d'Arlay Rosé
    'Les Pavillons'

Château d'Arlay
Château d'Arlay Red Macvin

SAVOIE

DOMAINE DE MÉJANE

73250 Saint Jean de la Porte
T 04 79 71 48 51
F 04 79 28 66 94
e domainedemejane@orange.fr
w www.domaine-de-mejane.com

The cellars are open from
Monday to Saturday, from 9 am
to 12 noon and 2 pm to 6 pm;
on Sundays by appointment

WINES

AOC Roussette de Savoie
AOC Vin de Savoie
    Chardonnay
AOC Vin de Savoie Jacquère

AOC Cuvée Plaisir de Vivre:
    Méthode Traditionnelle
Cuvée Douce Vie

AOC Rosé de Savoie

AOC Saint Jean de la Porte
    Mondeuse
AOC Vin de Savoie Gamay
AOC Vin de Savoie Persan
Cuvée Angélise
Pinot Cuvée Christiane

THE RHÔNE VALLEY

JEAN-LOUIS CHAVE

37 Avenue du Saint-Joseph
07300 Mauves
T 04 75 08 24 63
F 04 75 07 14 21

WINES

Hermitage Blanc
Hermitage Blanc Vin de Paille

Ermitage Rouge Cuvée Cathelin
Hermitage Rouge
St Joseph Rouge

DOMAINE DE L'ORATOIRE
SAINT MARTIN

84290 Cairanne
T 04 90 30 82 07
F 04 90 30 74 27
e falary@wanadoo.fr
w www.oratoiresaintmartin.com

The cellars are open from
9 am to 12 noon and from 2 pm
to 6.30 pm; closed on Sundays
and on bank holidays

WINES

Cairanne Blanc 'Haut-Costias'
Cairanne Blanc 'Réserve
    des Seigneurs'

Côtes du Rhone rosé 'Oratoire
    Saint Martin'

Cairanne Rouge 'Cuvée
    Prestige'
Cairanne Rouge 'Haut
    Coustias'
Cairanne Rouge 'Réserve
    des Seigneurs'
Côtes du Rhône 'Le P'tit
    Martin'
Côtes du Rhône Rouge
    'Oratoire Saint Martin'
Cuvée Séraphine

CHÂTEAU FORTIA

Route de Bédarrides, BP 13
84230 Châteauneuf-du-Pape
T 04 90 83 72 25
F 04 90 83 51 03
e fortia@terre-net.fr
w www.chateau-fortia.com

The cellars are open from
Monday to Saturday, from
9 am to 12 noon and from 2 pm
to 6 pm; and on Sundays, from
2 pm to 6 pm

WINES

Château Fortia Châteauneuf
    du Pape

Château Fortia Cuvée du
    Baron Châteauneuf du Pape
Château Fortia Réserve
    Châteauneuf du Pape
Château Fortia Tradition
    Châteauneuf du Pape

PROVENCE

CHÂTEAU DE SAINT MARTIN

Route des Arcs
83460 Taradeau
T 04 94 99 76 76
F 04 94 99 76 77
e chateaudesaintmartin@
    wanadoo.fr
w www.chateaudesaintmartin.
    com

The cellars are open every
day in the summer, from 9 am to
1 pm and from 3 pm to 7 pm.
In the winter they are open from
9 am to 12 noon and from 2 pm
to 6 pm, except on Sundays

WINES

Château de Saint Martin,
    Cru Classé Cuvée Comtesse
    Vieilles Vignes

Château de Saint Martin,
    Cru Classé Bulles de Rose

Château de Saint Martin,
    Cru Classé Cuvée Comtesse
    Vieilles Vignes
Château de Saint Martin,
    Cru Classé Cuvée
    Eternelle Favorite
No. 2 du Château de Saint
    Martin

Château de Saint Martin,
    Cru Classé Cuvée Comte
    de Rohan Chabot
Château de Saint Martin,
    Cru Classé Cuvée Comtesse
    Vieilles Vignes
Château de Saint Martin, Cru
    Classé Vin Cuit de Provence
No. 2 du Château de
    Saint Martin

CHÂTEAU VANNIÈRES

83740 La Cadière d'Azur
T 04 94 90 08 08
F 04 94 90 15 98
e info@chateauvannieres.com
w www.chateauvannieres.com

WINES

Château Vannières, Bandol
    AOC, Blanc

Château Vannières, Bandol
    AOC, Rosé
Héritage de Vannières,
    Vin de Pays, Rosé

Château Vannières, Bandol
    AOC, Côtes de Provence
    Rouge
Château Vannières, Bandol
    AOC, Rouge
Héritage de Vannières,
    Vin de Pays, Rouge
Vintage de Vannières

MAS DE LA DAME

Chemin Départemental 5
13520 Les Baux de Provence
T 04 90 54 32 24
F 04 90 54 40 67
e masdeladame@masdeladame.
com
w www.masdeladame.com

Open to visitors all year round (except Christmas Day and New Year's Day) for wine and oil tastings, from Monday to Friday, from 8 am to 6 pm; Saturday and Sunday, from 9 am to 7 pm

WINES

Coin Caché Blanc
Cuvée Gourmande Blanc
La Stèle Blanc

Cuvée Gourmande Rosé
Rosé du Mas

Coin Caché Rouge
Cuvée Gourmande Rouge
Réserve Rouge
La Stèle Rouge
Le Vallon des Amants

CORSICA

CLOS CAPITORO

Pisciatella (route de Sartène)
20166 Porticcio
T 04 95 25 19 61
F 04 95 25 19 33
e relais@clos-capitoro.com
w www.clos-capitoro.com

WINES

Ajaccio Blanc
La Cuvée Louis Bianchetti
Blanc
La Grande Réserve Blanc

Ajaccio Rosé

Ajaccio Rouge
Cuvée Jean Bianchetti
Cuvée Réserve Rouge
Imperial Cyrnos Blanc
de Blancs

Vins doux:
Grenache-based Vins Doux
Naturels and dessert wines
made from Malvoisie

LANGUEDOC-ROUSSILLON

CHÂTEAU DE JAU

66000 Cases de Pène
T 04 68 38 90 10
w www.chateau-de-jau.com

The Grill de Jau Restaurant is open in the summer months:
T 04 68 38 91 38

WINES

Côtes du Roussillon Blanc
Jaja de Jau
Muscat de Rivesaltes

Côtes du Roussillon Rosé
Grand Roussillon
Jaja de Jau

Côtes du Roussillon Villages
Côtes du Roussillon Villages
Talon Rouge
Jaja de Jau

CHÂTEAU DE PENNAUTIER

Vignobles Lorgeril, BP 4
11610 Pennautier
T 04 68 72 65 29
F 04 68 72 65 84
w www.chateaudepennautier.
com

20 double or twin rooms (breakfast and dinner available on request)

The restaurant is open from Monday to Thursday, from 10 am to 6 pm; Friday and Saturday, from 10 am to 10 pm; and every day from 1 July to 31 August, from 10 am to 10 pm except Sundays and Mondays when it closes at 6 pm

WINES

Château de Pennautier, Château de Caunettes and Domaine de Garille:

Château de Pennautier Terroir
d'Altitude

Château de Pennautier Terroir
d'Altitude

*Château de Pennautier, Château de
Caunettes and Domaine de Garille:*
AOC Cabardès
Vins de Pays de la Cité de
Carcassonne
Vin de Pays d'Oc Cépages

Château et Moulin de Ciffre:
AOC Faugères
AOC Languedoc
AOC Saint Chinian

Domaine de la Borie Blanche:
AOC Minervois
AOC Minervois La Livinière

Mas des Montagnes:
AOC Côtes du Roussillon
Villages Caramany
AOC Côtes du Roussillon
Villages Latour de France
Côtes du Roussillon Maury

ABBAYE DE VALMAGNE

34560 Villeveyrac
T 04 67 78 06 09
F 04 67 78 02 50
e email info@valmagne.com
w www.valmagne.com

Open every day from 15 June
to 30 September, from 10 am to
6 pm; from 1 October to 14 June,
Monday to Friday, from 2 pm
to 6 pm and on Saturday and

Sunday, from 10 am to 6 pm;
closed on Tuesdays from
15 December to 15 February
and closed over Christmas
and New Year. Free tastings
on request

There is an annual music festival:
e festival@valmagne.com
T 04 67 78 47 30

WINES

Cuvée Bernard et Benoît
Cuvée Comte de Turenne
Vins de Pays des Collines de
la Moure

Cuvée Bernard et Benoît

AOC Coteaux du Languedoc,
Grès de Montpellier
Cuvée Bernard et Benoît
Cuvée Cardinal de Bonzi
Cuvée Comte de Turenne
Vins de Pays des Collines de
la Moure

THE SOUTH-WEST

CHÂTEAU DE SAURS

81310 Lisle sur Tarn
T 05 63 57 09 79
F 05 63 57 10 71
e email info@chateau-de-saurs.
com
w www.chateau-de-saurs.com

The cellars are open from
2 pm to 6 pm by appointment only

WINES

Château de Saurs AOC Gaillac
Chateau de Saurs AOC Gaillac
Blanc Doux

Chateau de Saurs AOC
Gaillac rosé

Château de Saurs AOC
Gaillac, including Réserve
Eliézer and La Pigario
Chateau de Saurs AOC
Gaillac Primeur

CHÂTEAU DE BÉLINGARD

24240 Pomport
T 05 53 58 28 03
F 05 53 58 38 39
e laurent.debosredon@
wanadoo.fr

The cellars are open on
weekdays from 8 am to 6 pm and
on Saturday from 10.30 am to
6 pm by appointment only

WINES

Bergerac, including Cuvée
Blanche de Bosredon
and Lyvress
Côtes de Bergerac, including
Cuvée Blanche de Bosredon
and Ortus
Côtes de Bergerac Moelleux
Monbazillac, including Cuvée
Blanche de Bosredon

Bergerac

Bergerac, including Cuvée
Alliance

BORDEAUX

CHÂTEAU BATAILLEY

33250 Pauillac
T 05 56 00 00 70
F 05 57 87 60 30

WINES

Château Batailley
Grand Cru Classé
Pauillac

CHÂTEAU DU TAILLAN

56 avenue de la Croix
33320 Le Taillan Médoc
T 05 56 57 47 00
F 05 56 57 47 01
e email chateaudutaillan@
wanadoo.fr
w www.chateaudutaillan.com

The winery is open every day, from 9 am to 6 pm. Guests will be welcomed either by a member of the family or by the winemaker. Tasting tour or gourmet tour from Monday to Saturday from 10 am to 6 pm and on Sunday, when a reservation is necessary. Lunch or dinner is available for 10 to 20 people. Throughout the year the château organizes workshops in association with the Medocaines

WINES

Château la Dame Blanche

Le Rosé du Taillan

Haut Medoc Cru Bourgeois

CHÂTEAU DE ROZIER

33330, Saint-Laurent-des-
Combes
T 05 57 24 73 03
F 05 57 24 67 77
For information on wine/tastings, please contact Jean-Philippe Saby: info@vignobles-saby.com

WINES

Château Rozier Saint
Emilion Grand Cru

CHÂTEAU LAFITE
ROTHSCHILD

33250 Pauillac
T 05 56 73 18 18
F 05 56 59 26 83
e visites@lafite.com
w www.lafite.com

Visits to the château and tastings by appointment only, with at least two weeks' advance notice. Professionals at 9 am and 10.30 am; individuals at 2 pm and 3.30 pm; closed on holidays, bank holidays and from August to the end of October

WINES

Carruades de Lafite, Pauillac
Château Lafite Rothschild
Premier Cru Classé,
Pauillac